A CHARTERHOUSE MISCELLANY 1939 AND 1999

By the same author

One Young Man's War (1939–1946)
The Girardot Family, Vols I & II

A Charterhouse Miscellany 1939 and 1999

Michael Bray

A Square One Publication

First published in 1999 by
Square One Publications
The Tudor House,
16 Church Street,
Upton on Severn,
Worcestershire WR8 0HT

British Library Cataloguing in Publication Data
is available for this book

ISBN: 1 899955 38 0

Typeset in 11pt Times by
Avon Dataset Ltd, Bidford on Avon B50 4JH

Printed in Great Britain by
Biddles Ltd, Kings Lynn, England

Contents

Acknowledgements

My thanks to Sir Ralph Gibson, to Mrs Mardall and Mrs Corke at Charterhouse, and many others, who have given me information and encouragement. My thanks also to Mr Eric Dobby for permission to quote from Bill Moss's books, and to use various photographs, and a very special thanks to Mrs Suzie Quinn, who has typed the book into her computer, from my written notes.

All proceeds from the sale of this book will be given to the "Ian Bray Fund", in memory of my nephew Francis Ian Richard Bray (Gownboys 1955–1960) who was accidentally drowned whilst sailing in Chichester Harbour in June 1998. The money in the Fund will be used to support Charterhouse Charities, such as the "Gownboys Fund".

As my contribution to the Fund, I have paid for the cost of publication.

The Gownboys Fund

The Gownboys Fund provides a Charterhouse education for the children of Old Gownboys who cannot otherwise afford it, and for pupils in Gownboys who, through some catastrophe, can no longer have all their fees paid. The fund does this by fee support and over the years it has enabled a series of successful pupils to benefit from, and contribute to, the House.

We, the Housemasters since the War, have seen the Fund in action, approve it heartily and wish it could do more, since there have always been more worthy applicants than the Fund can support.

To celebrate the centenary of the Gownboy Association Dinner this year, Sir Christopher Walford launched an Appeal to increase the Fund so that it will be able to continue its work over the next century.

Almost all of you will know Gownboys and Girls, perhaps good friends, who have been helped in the past, though their identity is kept secret. We know who they were, and, believe us, they were splendid people.

ROBERT POWELL
JOCK REITH
PETER GARDINER
JOHN PHILLIPS
CLIVE CARTER
RICHARD GILLIATT
JIM FREEMAN

Editorial

Congress

The Editors wish to thank sincerely both those who, many at great inconvenience, have written for this magazine, and those who, in refusing, gave us their wishes for our success.

We wish, too, to thank all who have, in any way, given us help in producing it.

Lastly, we would say this: *Congress* is to be published this once only – for O.Cs and members of Brooke Hall cannot be expected to contribute articles every year. However, some day, there may be another such magazine when there is a new generation of literary O.Cs.

I.W.S. MOSS
F.A.M. BRAY
R.B. GIBSON

June 1939

Editorial

A Charterhouse Miscellany 1999

Being retired gives one the opportunity to do things that may have been at the back of one's mind for many years, but for which there was little time or energy available.

This book was one of them, and it has given me much pleasure in looking back over sixty years, not "in anger", but with gratitude, to many people. I am hoping that it might stimulate some present Carthusians to do something similar to *Congress*, as there must be plenty of new material to work on, and they would find it very worthwhile.

As the father-in-law of a "Gowngirl", I also look forward to their literary talents contributing to a new publication.

F.A.M. Bray
Ferme Lasserre
Couloume-Mondebat
32160 Plaisance du Gers
France

March 1999

CHAPTER I

Congress Revisited

In the Spring of 1939, three Gownboys had the idea of producing a School Magazine, consisting of articles contributed by well known Old Carthusians, and people connected with Charterhouse.

The three Gownboys were Bill Moss, Ralph Gibson, and myself. I think that the original idea was Bill's, and certainly, his enthusiasm carried the project along.

For Bill and myself, who were the same age, it was our last Quarter at Charterhouse, and we were then going out into the big world, but Ralph was eighteen months younger, and so would stay on, until he went up to Oxford.

We drew up a list of people, whom we could think of, and who, in our opinion, seemed to have had interesting lives or experiences, and wrote to them, asking them to contribute something for the proposed magazine.

It was to be called CONGRESS, "a coming together of . . . persons belonging to a particular body", and would be published, in the Summer Quarter of 1939, for one edition only.

A surprising number of the people written to, not only replied, but wrote articles, and some of these articles are still, in my opinion, interesting, even after sixty years.

With the articles that we had received, we put the magazine together, sold advertising space to local shops and retailers who supported the School, arranged for the printing, and had it all ready for sale on O.C. day 1939.

I cannot remember how many copies were printed but the completed magazine comprised some seventy pages of foolscap size, with some photographs, and was nicely bound, and sold for the vast sum of one shilling!

With the money from the sales, and from the advertising revenue, we just about covered our costs, but to us, it was our first business venture, and as it turned out, our first publishing venture.

It was very exciting.

Luckily, a copy of the magazine is in the School Archives, and I was able to re-read it, and decided to reproduce several of the articles in this book, and then to look back at the lives and careers of the three young editors, that were just beginning, to try and judge how they measured up to the older generations, who had contributed to the first CONGRESS, and who had inspired them, at the time.

Having sent out our letters, one of the first replies was a refusal, from Robert Graves, the author and poet, who wrote as follows:

> **Dear Mr Editor**
> Sorry: I have no story and don't write articles and the chief connexion that I have with the school is a recurrent nightmare that I am back there again: as a sort of supernumerary monitor at Gownboys – a great embarrassment to myself, the housemaster, the buttery-boys and my fellow-monitors. I tried to lay this nightmare two years ago by a visit to the house; but it was all so exactly the same as in 1914 even to the dirty marks of footballs on the ceiling of Hall *in July* that I got a very queer feeling from it and would not repeat the visit for anything. It is just twenty-five years ago that I was writing exactly your sort of letter on exactly the same letter-paper to literary O.Cs., asking them to contribute to a special number of the *Grey Friar*. I didn't really care whether

or not they sent anything – it was just part of the Editorial game – and was greatly surprised when they did. It was not yet clear to me how difficult it was for them to refuse. Remember this in 1964, when you get a letter yourself on Gownboy notepaper – from yourself, it will seem – asking for a contribution to (? ? ?); and follow the example of

Yours sincerely . . .
R. Graves

Readers of Graves' autobiography "Goodbye to All That" will understand his views of Charterhouse, pre World War I. I gave the original of this classic refusal, to the Charterhouse Archives, some years ago.

CONGRESS 1939

Contents

by Commander B. G. Scurfield R
STANDING ON THE CORNER, by Michael Standing
80 DEGREES N., by D. B. Keith R
THE WORLD LONG DISTANCE RECORD FLIGHT,
by Sqn. Ldr B. K. Burnett R

REMINISCENCE
A MEMORY OF CHARTERHOUSE,
by C. Aubrey Smith R
A LETTER FROM MR. PENNY, by Richard Goolden

POLITICS
WHAT GERMAN YOUTH IS BEING TAUGHT,
by G. A. Rowan-Robinson R
IMPRESSIONS OF FASCIST ITALY, by F. A. M. Bray
WHITHER GERMANY, by A. W. Tressler R

ARTICLES
THOMAS DAY, by Sir Samuel Scott R
BOGEY, by Henry Longhurst R
MEDICINE AS A CAREER, by Sir E. Farquhar Buzzard

TRAVEL
TUNISIAN SCENES, by Henry Baerlein R
A PLANTER IN JAMAICA, by Capt. John Blagrove
THE KINGDOM OF SIAM, by W. A. M. Doll

MISCELLANEOUS
TEN YEARS IN CHARTERHOUSE SPORT
PHOTOCRIME

R = Reprinted in 1999 in "A Charterhouse Miscellany, 1939 and 1999"

My Flight into the Soviet Union

by Brian Grover

A year ago my wife and I had almost despaired of ever meeting again. We had not seen each other for four years. She was a Soviet Citizen and the mountains of Red Tape on the road to her release from Soviet citizenship stood as unscaleable as ever, despite all our efforts in Moscow and in London.

We still corresponded freely through the post, and this kept hope alive. It seemed unbelievable that I was to be barred for ever from a wife whose letters took only three days to reach me, but I began to realise that I must take some steps outside of the usual diplomatic channels in order to achieve our reunion.

Somehow I must get back into the U.S.S.R. myself, and this was no easy matter because re-entry into the Soviet Union was forbidden me, and the Soviet frontier is the most closely guarded frontier in the world. If I succeeded merely in creeping across the line, I would be arrested and immediately sent back ignominiously. I must get deep into the country, if possible, right into Moscow itself, before being arrested. To fly in there in cloudy weather seemed to offer the best chance of doing this.

I must first learn to fly. I took a course of instruction at Heston School, and after eleven hours of dual instruction I accomplished the terrifying first solo flight.

My plans must be kept an absolute secret, for were any official to get wind of my intentions, all would be lost. I did not breathe a word to my closest neighbours or relatives; on the contrary, I went to great pains to throw them off the scent. Looking back now, I have to admit that some of my subterfuges were reprehensible, but you must remember how much I had at stake, and now that the attainment of my objective seemed to be within the bounds of possibility, nothing was to stand in my way. Before I actually set off I gave out that I was going away for a fortnight's golfing holiday in Scotland, and I told my people not to expect a letter from me, as I dislike writing. For the past sixteen years I had lived abroad almost continuously, working in various parts of the world where jobs offered, so that apart from relatives and near neighbours, I had few friends in London.

All my spare days I used to snoop around Flying Clubs and aerodromes, looking over aeroplanes for sale, and I eventually picked on an eighty horse Swallow. It was rather slow, but it was a sturdily built machine in good running order, and it had the great advantage of seven hours petrol capacity. I eventually closed with the dealer for the remarkably low figure of £173. This was my first stroke of luck.

Every night, and far into the small hours of the morning I used to pore over the route I would follow. The guiding consideration of secrecy decided me to go via Stockholm. The obvious route was through Poland and Latvia; unfortunately both of these States insist on knowing all about your business before they will admit you into their territory. So I thought it wiser to plan my route through Holland, Germany and Sweden, where I should be asked no embarrassing questions.

I read all I could lay my hands on about Air Navigation and weather conditions, and I realised that I should have to engage a professional airman to pilot me as far as Stockholm. It was one thing to be able to make circuits round Heston Aerodrome, but quite another to navigate my aeroplane across the Channel and from one Continental Air Port to another in the unfavourable weather which is usual in November. So I put an advertisement in one of the Air Periodicals, and I was lucky enough to get into touch with a first-class man who happened to be free at the moment, and who agreed to accompany me for expenses only.

In order to qualify for an Air Ministry "A" Licence, I had to complete three hours of solo flying, and pass certain prescribed flying tests. I had to undergo a rigorous medical examination, and also pass an oral exam. on the Air Regulations. By the 30th of October I had finished the last of my tests. On the 4th of November I got my actual "A" Licence from the Air Ministry, and on the same day my pilot and I pushed off in the Swallow for Stockholm.

We crossed the Channel and picked up the French coast at Cape Gris Nez, followed the coast line to Calais and circled the Semaphore Station there. This is the usual procedure to show that one has crossed the Channel safely. We then made a bee-line for Amsterdam, which we reached without further incident late in the afternoon. That was the first hop of our journey. Another four days brought us to Stockholm; here I had to wait for cloudy weather, and I spent the time completing the plans for my get-away.

I bought a complete outfit of duplicate baggage at the local Woolworths, to lcavc about in my hotel bedroom before my departure, so to make it appear that I was coming back. I bought a rucksack, a suit of pyjamas, hair brush, tooth brush, and shaving kit, all for a very few shillings. I wrote a short explanatory letter to my people in England, a similar letter to my wife in Moscow, and a note to my pilot, whom I had, of course, to abandon. Above all, I did not want the Aerodrome Authorities to search for me. I left my Pilot £20 for his return passage to England, and a sum to cover our hotel bill.

In the luggage locker of the Swallow I stowed a haversack full of kit and a thermos full of hot coffee. Every day I took a short flight so as to keep my hand in, and every evening I filled up thc fuel and oil tanks so as to be ready for immediate departure, the moment the weather was right.

Every morning I was up at daybreak to have a look at the weather. For many years I have made a habit of opening my Bible at random every morning, and reading a few verses. On the 13th November I started reading the sixth chapter of the Second Epistle to the Corinthians. The second verse is as follows:-

"I have heard thee in a time accepted, and in the day of salvation have I succoured thee: behold, now is the accepted time: behold, now is the day of salvation."

It was just getting light, and I saw immediately that the conditions were ideal for my illegal flight; there was practically no wind, and the sky was covered with a thick layer of Strata Cumulus. Here was my chance at last! I scattered the Woolworth baggage carefully around the room, left the note to my pilot in the hotel reception office, posted the other letters and took a taxi to the aerodrome.

I wheeled the Swallow out of the hangar and gave her the once over to make sure that all was in order, got permission from the Control Officer to take off and make a short circuit of the aerodrome; I gave myself contact, swung the prop myself, the engine started up first swing. Needless to say I did not make the promised circuit, but pushed straight on up, and thanks to the poor visibility was soon out of sight. At 1000 feet I entered dense cloud and I had to climb through a total thickness of 2,500 feet of cloud before I caught the first faint rays of the sun. A few moments later I was in bright sunshine, and the heavy cloud-bank spread out below me like a blanket, as far as the eye could see, in all directions. If only this keeps on all day, I thought, and if only the engine does not let me down, there is just a chance that I may get through.

My dread of exposure had prompted me not to ask for aviation maps for the course to Moscow. In any case they would have been quite useless under the existing conditions. In Stockholm I bought a plain schoolroom map, for which I paid about eighteen-pence. I drew a straight line from Stockholm to Moscow and the angle between this line and the meridian gave my compass bearing; I made no correction for drift, as it was impossible for me to know either the speed or direction of the wind, being, as I was, without sight of the earth.

My machine had an enclosed cockpit, and even at 10,000 feet it was nice and warm; I flew at this height so as to minimise the risk of being heard from the ground. Hour after hour I kept steadily on, holding the Swallow rigidly on her course, wondering vaguely how far I had got and what sort of reception I should get when the time came to land. I had taken off from Stockholm at 8.30 a.m. and by 2.30 the sun was sinking rapidly, and I saw that it would soon be dark, moreover my petrol was getting low. By 2.45 I had reached the top of the clouds. Five minutes of blind flying brought me down through the clouds again, and to my great relief I saw land below me. The country was well wooded, but it did not take long to pick out a large stubble field which looked suitable for a landing. I circled it twice quite low, peering out of the cockpit. It looked O.K. and I could see no ditches or tree stumps. I made a most successful landing, and felt thankful to be back safe on mother earth again. The time was exactly 3 o'clock. I switched off the engine – it had not missed a beat during the six-and-a-half hours since the start. There was a layer of ice on the front rim of my wings about three-quarters-of-an-inch thick; I think it must have formed as I came down through the clouds.

That evening, when I checked up my position on my map, I found that I was almost dead on my pencilled course and only about 100 miles short of Moscow. I had covered a distance of 650 miles, of which more than 200 were over the sea. My flying time was 6½ hours, so that the average land speed was 100 miles per hour. As the air speed of the Swallow is only 82 m.p.h. I must have had an 18 m.p.h. tail wind.

I had landed in a Soviet Collective Farm and was soon surrounded by village children, and later, by their parents. I told the President of the Farm that as I was a foreigner, he should let the police know of my arrival. I spent the night very comfortably at the farm and early the next morning a party of political police arrived. They made a very thorough examination of the Swallow and then took me by easy stages to Moscow, which we reached at noon on the following day. I was taken straight to Lubianka, which is the Headquarters of the Soviet Political Police.

The officer in charge of my escort got out of the car and went into the massive, grim-looking building, whilst I was kept waiting in the car outside. After about 30 minutes an official came up to the car and told me to get out and follow him; my escort followed close on my heels. We went through three sets of doors, each guarded by an armed sentry. Each sentry examined the Pass and I and every member of my escort had to go up to him singly, and whisper our full names in his ear before he would allow us to pass through. Finally, we came to a lift. I had to go in first into an inner compartment, where I was shut in alone. The door had an eye-hole in it through which I was watched. The lift stopped and I was led along a carpeted corridor. We stopped outside room number 728.

The room was a huge one, the size of a lounge in an expensive hotel. I noticed immediately that it was beautifully furnished – concealed lighting – a long Kashan rug on the polished floor and at the far end, behind a massive mahogany desk, sat a police officer. On a table at his side were nine telephones, but he must have told the exchange not to disturb him, because none of them rang during the interview. This was the moment I had visualised for the past ten weeks, and I knew that the next few minutes would decide not only my own fate, but my wife's also. There were a dozen assistants in the room, all standing and they all stared at me in silence as I walked up to the man at the mahogany desk. "Sit down," he said. "Is it true that you have flown into Soviet Territory without even obtaining permission?" "It is," I said. "That is a serious matter," he said. "What on earth did you do it for?" "I came on purpose to talk to you personally about my wife," I said. "She is here in Moscow, and I want either to stay with her here or else to take her away with me abroad."

For the next hour-and-a-half I was kept busy telling my story and answering their numerous questions. The original severe attitude of the Chief changed to one of curiosity. "I shall have to detain you," he said finally "my subordinates will question you in detail – we shall soon know whether you are telling the truth."

My cross-examination in Lubianka continued with intervals over a period of about three weeks. I was called up for questioning every three or four days, and I used to look forward to these interviews as a pleasant interlude in the monotonous life in my cell. I asked to be allowed to write to my wife, but I was told that no political prisoner could receive or send any communication prior to trial.

I was in Lubianka jail for seven weeks altogether. It is a model prison. On arrival, one's person, one's clothing and belongings are closely examined: money, valuables and dangerous articles like knives, razors and mirrors, are taken for safe keeping, and a formal receipt is given: you are then escorted to your cell through long, brightly lit corridors. The floors are tiled and well carpeted, and the walls and ceilings distempered in white or plain colours. The whole establishment radiates an atmosphere of warmth and comfort and of meticulous and clock-like efficiency. As far as material conditions were concerned, every reasonable comfort was provided, but the weary weeks dragged on and I still had no clue as to the outcome of my quest.

At length, on December 27th, a copy of the Indictment was handed to me. It contained a summary of the evidence and it defined the charges against me for which I was to be brought to trial. An official called to let me know that a date for my trial had been fixed for four days ahead, he asked if I desired the services of a Defence Counsel, and he gave me the names of the two foremost advocates in the Union. I knew neither of them, so I picked the first on the list, a Mr Komodov. I had a short talk with him before the trial. He had read up the case, but he told me that as I was pleading "Guilty", he could only appeal for a light sentence.

My trial took place in the Moscow City Courts on the afternoon of the 31st of December. I anticipated a very quiet affair, almost in camera, so it was a surprise to be led into a large hall full of people. The front row packed by the British Embassy, and behind them a score of Newspaper Correspondents. A bell announced the arrival of the judges, one woman and two men. The President was quite young and exceptionally well groomed. Everyone stood up as the judges entered the court and filed into their places on the bench.

The President asked me if I acknowledged the authority and jurisdiction of the court. He then read out the indictment. Next, he put a series of questions which I answered in almost identical phrases to those I had used when replying to the police investigators. The President asked his colleagues on the bench if they wished to ask the accused any further questions, and my counsel was allowed the same privilege. He then made his speech in mitigation of the sentence.

He pointed out that the Soviet Government guarded its frontiers against the intrusion of spies from foreign countries, but that the examination of my case had disclosed no political motives. On the contrary, I had come at great personal risk and expense to draw attention to my domestic affairs. Inasmuch as the Soviet State frowned upon frivolous attachments between foreigners and Russian women, so much the more did they respect and approve the genuine devotion of a married couple. Here was a young man who had become dissatisfied with capitalism and had entered the Soviet Union to engage in creative work. His record was exemplary, and whilst he must know that the Soviet frontier cannot be violated with impunity, he nevertheless had a right to expect a just verdict from a Proletarian Court.

The judges retired to consider their decision. After forty minutes the President announced the sentence: My aeroplane was to be confiscated, I was to pay a fine of 1,500 roubles – the equivalent of £60 sterling – or alternatively, to undergo a month's imprisonment, and I was not to re-enter Soviet Territory for another five years.

Counsel advised me not to appeal. I agreed to this: but I was bitterly disappointed that nothing in the verdict had any bearing on my wife's fortunes. By Soviet Law no sentence can be put into effect until four days have elapsed after its pronouncement, so as to give the convicted man ample time to frame an appeal. I did not know of this and immediately upon my return to prison, I told the superintendent that I wanted to pay the fine, to be set at liberty at once and allowed to go abroad with my wife.

At 10 p.m. on the 4th of January, the warder told me to dress and leave the cell, taking everything with me. All my other belongings which had been held in safe custody were returned to me, and checked up against the receipt. I was then taken to the Governor's office.

In a quiet voice he addressed me as follows: "Here is a copy of your sentence. Hold on to it carefully. You will have to show it if you are asked for your identification paper. Here is the balance of your money after paying the fine imposed by the court. Please sign the receipt for it. You are now a free man, and if you go to the Yaroslavsky Station you will find your wife waiting for you. She will be there till midnight. You can just about make it if you hurry. No. 42 tram is the best from here. If you miss your wife at the station, take a train to Bolshevo. This is her address" – he gave me a slip of paper with the number of the cottage and the street name written on it – "You must both of you, leave the country within 72 hours. Well, that is all, I think," he said, "Good-bye and Good Luck to you."

You can perhaps imagine my delight. First, I was to see my wife almost immediately, and then we were to go back to England together. The Soviets had done the handsome thing, and I had got my way at last.

1999

Brian Grover was in Hodgsonites, and left the school to become a civil engineer in 1919. After his remarkable adventure to get his wife out of Russia, he planned to start a new life in Uganda.

However, the last address that the School Archives have, was in South Africa.

Jan Grootboom

by Lord Baden-Powell

Jan Grootboom was a Zulu by birth, but having lived much with white men, as a hunter and guide, he had taken to wearing ordinary clothes and could speak English well; but within him he had all the pluck and cunning of his race.

For scouting against the Matabele it was never wise to take a large party, since it would be sure to attract attention, whereas by going alone with one man, such as Grootboom, one was able to penetrate their lines and lie hid almost among them, watching their disposition and gaining information as to their numbers, supplies, and whereabouts of their women and cattle.

Now, every night was spent at this work – that is to say, the night was utilised for creeping to their positions, and one watched them during the day. But it was impossible to do this without leaving footmarks and tracks, which the sharp eyes of their scouts were not slow to discover, and it very soon dawned upon them that they were being watched, and consequently they were continually on the look-out to waylay and capture us.

One night Grootboom and I had ridden to the neighbourhood of one of the enemy's camps, and were lying waiting for the early dawn so that we could discover exactly where they were located.

It was during the hour before sunrise that, as a rule, the enemy used to light their fires for cooking their early morning food. One could thus see exactly their position, and could rectify one's own, so as to find a place where one could lie by during the day and watch their movements.

On this occasion the first fire was lit, and then another sparked up, and yet another, but before half a dozen had been lighted Grootboom suddenly growled under his breath:

"The swine – they are laying a trap for us."

I did not understand at the moment what he meant, but he said:

"Stop here for a bit and I will go and look."

He slipped off all his clothing and left it lying in a heap, and stole away in the darkness practically naked. Evidently he was going to visit them to see what was going on.

The worst of spying is that it makes you always suspicious, even of your best friends. So, as soon as Grootboom was gone in one direction, I quietly crept away in another, and got among some rocks in a small kopje, where I should have some kind of a chance if he had any intention of betraying me and returning with a few Matabele to capture me.

For an hour or two I lay there, until presently I saw Grootboom creeping back through the grass – alone.

Ashamed of my doubts, I therefore came out and went to our rendezvous, and found him grinning all over with satisfaction while he was putting on his clothes again. He said that he had found as he had expected, an ambush laid for us. The thing that had made him suspicious was that the fires, instead of lighting up all over the hillside at different points about the same time, had been lighted in steady succession one after another, evidently by one man going round. This struck him as suspicious, and he then assumed that it was done to lead us on, if we were anywhere around, to go and examine more closely the locality.

He had crept in towards them by a devious path, from which he was able to perceive a whole party of the Matabele lying low in the grass by the track which we should probably have used in getting there, and by which they would have pounced upon us and captured us.

To make sure of this suspicion, he crept to a point near their stronghold, and coming from there he got in among them, finding out what was their intention with regard to ourselves, and also what were their plans for the near future. Then, having left them, and walked boldly back towards their stronghold, he crept away amongst some rocks and rejoined me.

His was an example of the work of a field spy which, although in a way it may be cunning and deceitful, at the same time demands the greatest personal courage and astuteness. It is something greater than the ordinary bravery of a soldier in action, who is carried on by the enthusiasm of those around him under the leadership of an officer, and with the competition and admiration of his comrades.

The pluck of the man who goes out alone, unobserved and unapplauded, and at the risk of his life, is surely something more admirable.

1999

Lord Baden Powell was born in 1857, the seventh son of the Revd. Baden Powell, F.R.S., a professor at Oxford. He went to Gownboys in 1870, and to Girdlestoneites from 1874 to 1876.

He joined the Army and served in Zululand, Ashanti and Matebeleland, and was the defender of Mafeking, 1899–1900, in the South African War.

He started the Boy Scout Movement in 1908, and was the World Chief Scout in 1920.

Created Lord Baden Powell in 1929, he received the O.M. in 1936, and was President of the O.C. Club, 1923–5. He died in Kenya in 1941.

Salute to Old Masters

or Are Schoolmasters What They Were?

by W.C. Sellar (Housemaster of Daviesites 1939)

Co-author of "1066 and All That"

When my grandfather was 80 years of age he used to toboggan downstairs on an old tin try. He suffered a good deal from rheumatism and found tobogganing the easiest way of reaching the ground floor. You must not discredit this statement: it is the unvarnished truth.

As it happens, my grandfather was not a schoolmaster, but I always think he missed his true vocation; for is not that exactly the kind of way that schoolmasters of the true old breed behaved? Certainly most of them, if one can believe the stories told by their pupils, were 80 years of age.

In those far-off days you could never mistake a schoolmaster for a member of any other profession. Schoolmasters wore outlandish clothes; they carried the birch and muttered Greek into their beards as they prowled about the town. Nobody, least of all a boy, would have been surprised to see a schoolmaster sliding downstairs on a tin tray.

Today schoolmasters are different: they are often indistinguishable from other men. Quite a number of them are not even poor.

On the whole, they are nice well-bred men with a cultured taste in pictures, radiograms and the like; they buy new motor cars every second year; they eat like gentlemen; they send their trousers to be cleaned and pressed; they possess more than one neck-tie each; they are often liberal reformers and steadfastly deplore the old defeatist notion that "boys will be boys".

That is all very well: no doubt they are good clean specimens of Western civilization and a good example to their boys. But what I want to know is, are they really *schoolmasters*? Are they repressed geniuses? Are they uncertified lunatics (as, clearly, their predecessors were) with some useless but magnificent enthusiasm to impart? I do not know one of them who collects spittoons or plays cricket in galoshes. Many of them can hardly recognise a Greek quotation. As a matter of fact, they *wash*!

In the old days, when our fathers and grandfathers were at school, schoolmasters did not wash. Of course not: they were not

Old Grouch mooing a paradigm

paid to. And if you can't afford to wash, you spend your hours of leisure in some other way.

My uncle used to tell me about "old Farquharson", who dug a hole in the ground. He dug it every afternoon, summer and winter, for 46 years and died, as he would have wished, at the bottom of it. For the first 20 years the hole got deeper and deeper. He wanted to see how deep he could make it. He installed ropes and pulleys and buckets, and bailed out the water. He reinforced the walls of it. He made a primitive sort of gas mask and went down into the pit every afternoon from 2.30 to 3.30. After 20 years he decided that the circumference at the top was too small – *So he filled it in and started all over again with a wider circumference.*

It certainly was a *hole* by the time old Farquharson had finished with it. And when people asked him what it was for, he used to mutter: "*Facilis descensus Averno*. It's a hole in the ground, I'll trouble you, and I wish to meet the man who can make a better one."

There was never any doubt that Farquharson was a schoolmaster. Nobody would have mistaken him for a stockbroker or a barrister. It matters very little what he taught the boys in school hours: actually, I believe, he taught them Latin grammar. But when, in later years, they met as Old Boys on the Afghan Frontier, they said: "It's wonderful to think of old Farquharson digging away at that hole." In fact, he gave the Old Boys something to think about – and there are many Old Boys who need that. The Old Boys in Australia, of course, had no end of fun betting on the day when old Farquharson would pop up under their feet.

* * *

Then there was "old Grouch" (were these men ever young?). He had been at Oxford with Farquharson and, according to my uncle, despised him for a pedant. Grouch dug no holes in the ground. He spent most of his leisure trying to *photograph Centipedes*. He was only 5-ft. tall, which perhaps gave him an unfair advantage in this respect. But there are no schoolmasters of only 5-ft. nowadays: they are all average men, catering for the average boy, about whom they have collected reliable statistics. They have no statistics about the average Centipede.

Besides being only 5-ft. high, Grouch had a scarifying red beard which shot out from his chin almost at right angles to his face. The beard had a hole in the middle of it, through which he used to pass a ruler gently up and down as he recited Greek paradigms to his form in a low, cow-like voice. I have in my possession a rapid pen-and-ink sketch, done by my uncle and dated 1879, entitled "Old Grouch mooing Biβλιο$^{\rho}_{0}$κω." It is reproduced here by kind permission of my uncle.

Another characteristic of the Old Masters was, I think, their magnificent aloofness about material things. If there was only one bath among 50 boys, what was that to them? If the benches were broken in the boys' Common Room, well – the boys could stand. I remember hearing of one house where the boys were not allowed to sit down until they had been at the school two years, – and owing to the prevalence of corporal punishment in those days, there was little inclination to complain.

Even when I was at school myself, twenty years ago, the chief indoor recreation was "dormitory rugger", a game which the Housemaster used to come and watch. The game was played with a new boy's sponge-bag, and a try was scored by hurling oneself (clutching the sponge-bag) into the stone fire-place at the end of the dormitory. Full points could be scored by kicking the sponge-bag (and if possible the new boy) out of the window.

As for the problem of feeding the boys, it was simple enough: The parents paid the Housemaster a boarding fee by way of *couvert* (as the restaurants call it) and then gave the boy enough pocket money to buy his own food. The Old Masters had a certain horse sense: they knew that if one gave the boys nothing to eat, they could not very well complain of the quality of the food.

And they believed in self-determination. They allowed the boys to make their own rules to an extent that would horrify even the most up-to-date free educationists today. Thus, in some schools a new boy had to wear all his clothes back-to-front for the first year, and no one might carry a mackintosh or an umbrella until he reached the Sixth Form. In others, all juniors were compelled to tie their bootlaces in granny knots at the back of the boot, while fellows with football or boxing colours could keep their hands in their pockets in Chapel and were exempted from taking off their hats to Clergymen or Masters' wives. It was, I think, universally recognised that no boy in the Cricket XI need do any work.

With such rules and privileges the Old Masters were, one must suppose, in perfect sympathy. Or, more likely perhaps, in their indifference to material things, they simply did not notice. Many of them, after all, wore their own clothes inside-out and upside-down.

* * *

And yet, there is one uncomfortable thought which haunts me:

Oh wad some Power the giftie gie us
To see oursels as others see us . . .

We who buy our new motor cars, and eat like gentlemen, and send our trousers to be cleaned and pressed, we *average* pedagogues of 5 ft. 10½-ins., – do we, as we sit in our class-rooms droning away about Pitt and Palmerston, and the longer paradigm of *pouvoir*, appear to the young generation to be as bemused, as eccentric, as utterly unpresentable in polite society as "old Farquharson" and "old Grouch" once seemed to my uncle and his contemporaries? Do they think we are all, at least in our mental habits, over 80 years of age? Is it possible that the unwritten title of that little pen-and-ink sketch which I found the other day under a desk, might have been "Old S—, mooing the paradigm of *pouvoir*"?

1999

W.C. Sellar came to the School in OQ 1932, was Housemaster Daviesites from LQ 1939, and died at Charterhouse in 1951.

Beauty and The Beast

by Ben Travers

Old Man Cassim, of Hamadan Town, Persia, had two daughters, and their names were Fatima and Beauty; which sounds a bit of a backhander for Fatima at the outset, but she made it up to herself in other ways all right. For instance –

When this Cassim, who was some sort of commercial, it appears, had to set off one bright morning on a round of business and a camel, he says rashly to the two girls:

"Now girls, when Poppa comes back from Bagdad, just what sort of souvenir would you be tickled to find under the sponge-bag in the off corner of the grip?"

"A diamond necklace," says Fatima without hesitation, having had enough of the old, squashed packets of Turkish delight which the old man had wished on her hitherto, "a diamond necklace will be in the bag, dad, I guess."

Cassim counters this with the even older wheeze about "Guess again," and cocks the inquisitive eyelid up at Beauty.

Now Beauty was modest and sentimental and a bit of a poor fish, it seems.

"A rose," simpers Beauty; and "Thank Allah only one of 'em takes after their mother," says Cassim, and straddles his hump and hits the horizon.

Four days later found the camel tethered on his knees and

eating thorns sideways in the stable of the "Bull and Bulbul," Bagdad, and old man Cassim sampling the salted almonds in the tap-room.

There was another bagman in the bar, by name Suleyman or something; and, after passing the time of day and exchanging the blessings of Allah with Suleyman and the bar-houri, old Cassim ups his sample-grip and goes forth to see whether he can't unload a new line in gents' shirtings on Mosaids, Ltd., of High Street, Bagdad.

Well, Cassim happened to catch the Mosaid buyer in melting mood and a bit low in shirtings, and booked about two and a half camel-loads of dry goods, and clinched the deal with a couple of rounds of wet goods, and beat it out of the store so full of buck that darned if he didn't go off and buy the necklace for Fatima.

It may not have been exactly a diamond necklace, but it was a good enough one to make the bar-houri at the "Bull" say, "Oh my, I reely couldn't!" and to cool down to a point below freezing when she discovered that she wasn't intended to, anyway.

But the bar-houri was on the right lines, for see what comes of being too modest. Old man Cassim was cross-legged on the hump again, and with the carrot in front of the camel's nose pointing the path for home, before he smote himself on the turban and said:

"There! By the beard of the Prophet, I've forgotten Beauty's rose. Never mind; I'll say I dropped it in the road, or give her the carrot instead."

But just then he happened to pass a garden, and, being good and high on the hump, could see over the wall; whereupon his optic nerve gave notice of a whole bunch of roses, each one of them as big as the rose you can see being offered to the girl with the high waist by the young man with the side-whiskers and tight black pants in the picture in the spare bedroom. So Cassim instinctively woa'ed his camel and did a trapeze act into the garden.

By the time he'd hotstuffed about two dozen roses and had

stung his fingers on a nettle, he was ripe for the hump once more, and humpwards was indeed retreating – but no, he didn't.

For, from behind a bush, sounded a noise which seemed a sort of mixture between the eleven thirty Southern Railway express starting off at twelve and the bit where they sing the chorus in the coon band gramophone record, and out comes the beast.

"Hallo, lunch," says the beast.

Old Cassim dry-shampoo'ed his hands and handed out an imitation of a minister caught kissing the parlourmaid.

"What magnificent roses, sir!" he says. "I just had to —" And so on. But he didn't pull anything over on the beast.

"Yes, aren't they just beautiful?" says the beast. "Don't go. This is great. I haven't had a good square man-meal in weeks. I'm through with goat-and-olive pudding. Hi, Mansoor!"

At which a great buck Ethiopian slave, about as big as your father when you're two, arrived on the scene and started smoothing the gravel with his forehead.

"Cut all that out," says the beast, "and show this gentleman to the kitchen."

Old Cassim therefore reluctantly decided to tell the truth.

"Beauty, eh?" says the dog-faced boy, getting interested. "Is this on the level? Well, I tell you what. You send along for this Beauty right away. If she isn't here by Saturday your name will be some word in French invented by the cook."

So Cassim went back to the wall and had a look-see up and down the road for a messenger, with Mansoor practising iron shots with his snickersnee in the immediate vicinity.

It so happened that friend Suleyman was homeward plodding his weary at about this hour. Cassim hails him from the fence and puts him sane to the situation.

"Bellevue, Fig Lane, Hamadan, is the address," he concludes. "You'll find Beauty there. Only get a move on," cries the desperate man.

Who is this sideshow who's got a hold of you, anyway?" inquires Suleyman.

"I can't rightly say", says Cassim. "But I guess it's one of these cases where a prince has fallen foul of a fairy and had his expression registered dog for him.

"Well, I fell foul of a fairy myself only last night in Baghdad," says Suleyman. "But she didn't come no disfigurements on me."

"She didn't have to, with your face," says Cassim. "I say, do make this exit. That camel shifts at about the speed of a cricket umpire coming out after the luncheon interval."

"Righto," says Suleyman. "Allah be with you. The beer's on you again next time."

With which Suleyman humped up and Cassim was taken along to the beast's castle and parked in the scullery.

Three days elapse, and just as Cassim is getting worried by the cook reading bits of a Mrs. Beeton aloud to himself in the kitchen, Beauty does a Jack-and-Jill landing off the camel into a raspberry bush in the drive and pushes into this high-class menagerie.

"Oh, good enough," says the beast at but a glance. "Recamel that father. She's here for keeps."

"You'll excuse me, sir," says Beauty, "but what's the game exactly? I'm not that sort of girl; and if you mistake yourself for Owen Nares, breathe on the mirror and rub lightly."

"You're going to remain here," says the beast, "until you say you love me."

"Gosh!" says Beauty. "And I've only brought one of everything."

On the first day that Beauty stayed there the beast gave her board and lodging, some glass bracelets, a Pomeranian, and one of those darn-fool little umbrellas that girls use nowadays.

"Now will you say you love me?" he asks.

"Shall I have to give the presents back if I say no?" asks Beauty.

"No," says he.

"Oh, what a cinch," says Beauty. "No."

Next day he gave her a rope of pearls and a Rolls-Royce and one of those big round boxes of chocolates tied up with ribbons like you see the dudes bring their sweeties on the pictures, and an order on the hatter's and everything.

"Love me now?" he asks.

"And quit this?" says Beauty. "No."

"Oh, is *this* the way your mental machinery functions over this outfit!" remarks the beast. "I've a mind to spank you good and hearty." With which he caught her by the neck and performed his noise, like he did at Father in the garden.

"My hero!" cries Beauty. "My great, beautiful, hairy, gorgeous cave-man! My luscious library subscriber's hope! The rough stuff goes. I love you."

This does the trick. Off flies his fur, and he's Ivor.

"I'm a handsome prince really," he explains. "Got a wicked witch's goat and was transmogrified into the dope fiend's nightmare until loved for myself alone."

"Oh, how sloppy!" says Beauty. "I liked you fierce. Still, there we are, and I suppose we'd better get married. It's no good my going home in a Rolls and saying it's just a Platonic affair."

"Fancy!" says Fatima, when Beauty got back home and published her particulars. "You, of all people. Quite romantic. Just as well it wasn't me perhaps. I'd most likely have loved him right away for the Pom and the umbrella and missed the Rolls. Besides, as a matter of fact, I've hopes of my own in another direction. That young caliph who's come to live at the corner of Cokernut Avenue. Only he's terribly backward. Say, Beauty! I wonder whether you could get your boy to tell you the name and address of that witch?"

1999

Benjamin Travers was born in 1886 and left Daviesites in 1904.

In WWI he was a Squadron Commander in the Royal Naval Air Service, but transferred to the R.A.F. in 1918. Awarded the A.F. Cross.

He was a dramatist, novelist, and author of a number of plays, novels and films.

In WWII, he rejoined the R.A.F. as a Squadron Leader. Awarded the C.B.E.

President of the O.C. Club in 1963.

Sea Shanty of a Bad Sailor

by A.W. Bird

Upon the rolling billow I could gaze
In wonder and in awe for days and days,
Or feast my fascinated eyes on lights
Reflected in the sea for nights and nights –
But from the solid shore I'd have you mark,
Not from the deck of some unstable barque.

1999

A.W. Bird, born 1876, left Gownboys in 1893. Became a chemical manufacturer.

WWI Captain, Royal Berkshire Regiment. He died in 1953.

High Failure

by John Grierson

John Grierson's interest in flying was first kindled by a book called "10,000 Things a Bright Boy Can Do," in which was described the construction of a glider. He started to build this at the age of fifteen, and added certain "improvements" of his own, such as an engine. Perhaps luckily for his health, the machine was not completed.

Having joined the R.A.F. he was sent to India, but, not liking the conditions there, sent in his resignation. When this was refused he took matters into his own hands and flew back to England, where he was placed under arrest. However, a week after he had been released he was notified that he had been "removed" from the R.A.F.

It was the possibility of an air route from England to America, via Iceland, that led him to make the flight of which he writes. Flying from Reykjavik to Angmagssalik he became lost and landed in a fjord on the coast of Greenland. It is in that fjord that the following narrative commences.

Softly the night fell and, glancing out of my cabin window, I could see an array of stars which seemed so near in the clear air that it looked as if I could stretch out my hand and touch the sky. By jove, I did feel cold. It was not so bad when the air was still, but every now and again a puff of wind came straight off the glacier penetrating the door-seams and the gaps in the windows. The old overalls and cleaning rags were powerless against it, and it cut my body just like a knife. Fortunately these puffs only lasted for about five minutes. After them silence fell, broken only by the babbling of the glacier stream. I reflected that, if I was going to live long aboard Robert Bruce, something would have to be done to defrigerate the atmosphere of the cabin.

I was almost dozing when suddenly I noticed a feeling of motion on the craft. It was one o'clock. On peeping out I saw that we were fully afloat and the tide was well in. With the aid of my torch I took my boots and socks off once more, to make my second and even longer plunge into the icy water. It was so clear that I could see the stones on the bottom plainly. My first task was to wade in to my two "anchors" and lift them up on to the floats. There was a thin skin of ice on the surface as I lowered

John Grierson and 'Robert Bruce'

myself, farther than I expected, on to the stony bottom: it *was* cold! The water was above my knees and the surface very uneven for walking. Following first one grass-line and then the other, I located the heavy stones, which I lifted with some difficulty on to the float-noses, staggering under the weight, over the sharp stones and in water at minus temperature. Luckily my feet were so numb that they would not feel the rough edges on which they were being placed. Again, with my torch I paddled across the fjord, pushing Robert Bruce towards a position of better shelter in the corner. We had to circumnavigate a couple of grounded growlers on the way to our goal, where it was necessary to dodge between boulders before running on to the beach. I took care to run aground stern first for two reasons: firstly, that it would facilitate getting off when I wanted to refloat, and secondly, because I expected any gale to blow from the glacier into the fjord, tending to press the machine on to the ground instead of off it as when headed into wind. Mine was not the orthodox procedure, but I know that the late Colonel G.L.P. Henderson once rode out a 90 m.p.h. gale in this manner when otherwise the machine would have been wrecked.

I lost no time in putting out my anchors so that I could return aboard and replace my footwear. Even by the light of my torch I could see that those feet of mine were redder than they had ever been before and, so far as feeling was concerned, they might have belonged to an Eskimo 20 fjords away. Rubbing with a handkerchief or bits of rag did not make much difference, so I banged them with the tool bag until they jolly well had to sit up and take notice. Almost as soon as I had got my boots on, I felt that we were afloat again. I had no idea of how much farther the tide had to run, but I was determined to keep pushing Robert Bruce up with it until we reached the high-water mark. So I clambered out on to the float armed with my boathook and used it as a punt pole.

I had to keep rearranging the anchors as we worked our way shorewards, steering clear of large stones and an occasional growler. We were beside a huge rock, trying to keep close to it for shelter, but without bumping the wing. There were plenty of things for me to watch. In fact, I was fully occupied all the time the tide rose, punting, arranging the anchors, keeping an eye on the wings by flashing the torch and looking out for obstructions ahead. Occasionally I would think that we had reached the final limit, only to find that we were afloat again the next minute. In the cold it seemed a tiresome process, though in reality, since I could not go to sleep, this job of work was a blessing. It occupied my thoughts and gave me a definite task on which to concentrate. Very nearly two hours after I had begun paddling, Robert Bruce grounded and was left high and dry on the shingle by the receding waters.

Back, in the cabin it seemed as cold as ever, and I made up my mind that, when I next went out, I should heat myself some cocoa with my Tommies' cooker. I tried very hard to sleep, though whether I did or not will always be uncertain, for by the time daylight had returned I could neither remember going off to sleep nor waking up. The floor of the cabin was so hard and I was so very cramped that I could not remain in the same position for more than five minutes at the utmost. These discomforts, combined with the intense cold, militated against slumber, and it is unlikely that I obtained more rest than dozing could give. Yet I persisted in trying to get repose so that I might be as fit as possible for whatever trials the morrow might bring forth. Presently, I felt that I would rather go out and stretch myself, for my limbs were aching and outside the sun was shining in a cloudless sky. But before leaving the cabin, I thought that it would be a good plan to try making it draught-tight, whilst the devastating effect of the chinks was still fresh in my memory. The best material I had with me consisted of black adhesive tape, and with my knife I carefully cut it into lengths. It stuck fairly well to the woodwork of the door-hinges, but took a lot of persuasion to "stay put" on the celluloid windows. However, I found that by careful application of cross-strips at suitable intervals an airtight joint could be made, though there was no possibility of its resistance to anything stronger than a gentle puff of wind. I engaged in this task with the meticulous care of one who knows that, little as the benefit may be, his work is the only thing which may in some small way improve his situation. Once again, since my midnight paddle, I was able to relax in toil that demanded concentration. Besides, the effect of the first shock was beginning to wear off. The outlook to-day was more cheerful and I was almost looking forward to trying the Greenland fishing with the line and hook which the Canadian Government had kindly forced me to carry.

Whilst still plying the adhesive tape, suddenly I heard a weird screaming noise, like the cry of some wild bird. It was so loud that I was convinced that it could not be my imagination, being played on by the stream. Yet I had never believed that there were big enough birds in Greenland to create such a volume of sound. Anyway, it wasn't worth while getting out of the cabin until I had finished the process of draught-proofing it, thought I. But again the scream was uttered, longer and louder than the last time. On second thoughts I decided that if this was a big bird, I ought to go and investigate: I must not miss any chance of stocking the larder and perhaps I could shoot this animal. As I jumped out, I heard the noise yet a third time, apparently coming from beyond a ledge of shingle. I ran forward towards it, supposing that I should see one or more huge birds circling. The next moment, to my unbelieving eyes, came the most unexpected and at the same time the most supremely joyful sight I have ever seen. It was a man running over the rocks towards me and making the weird screaming noise that had brought me out. I did hope he wouldn't be frightened of the seaplane and run away again as suddenly as he had appeared. But he came on, and following was a second, a third, a fourth and even a fifth. In a flash the whole situation had been changed. My flight could go on! Trembling with emotion, I felt tears coming to my eyes as I seized each Eskimo by the hand and rung it with a fervour, which only the saved can know. I tried to ask them where Angmagssalik was, and though they could speak no English, they pointed in the direction from which they had come.

I asked the Eskimos to stand in front of Robert Bruce for a photograph. To my surprise they did not display any signs of camera-shyness, and on this occasion it was I who behaved as if I had never seen a camera before. I forgot to adjust the focusing screw and this, combined with my shaking hand, produced a photograph which, as my reader can see, was anything but clearly defined. Almost as soon as I had taken the snap, I saw two more men coming over the rocks. One, I noticed, was wearing breeches, a white sweater, and a leather strap to support a pair of binoculars. Instead of the round Eskimo face, he had the longer Nordic type. I guessed that this fellow would be the leader of the expedition, probably a Dane, and therefore almost certain to speak English. As I shook his hand, he explained to me that it was a long time since he had last spoken English and that he had forgotten many words. But his talk was by no means so broken that it was unintelligible. First of all, I asked him to join the group by my machine so that I could take a photograph of the whole rescue party. I still did not focus, but the result was slightly better. The English speaker introduced himself as Pastor Rosing. He explained that they had seen me fly almost over the settlement heading west, and were astonished when I did not land. They had heard my S.O.S. signal so clearly that the wireless operator was certain that I could not be far off. The fact that I was in an ice-free fjord three miles from the sea where the coast ran east and west was also a useful clue. Originally, Rosing had set out with only five Eskimos, but they met a water-carrier who asked them where they were going. "Towards Sermilik," they replied (Sermilik being the great fjord to the west of the settlement which had been so full of ice that it had looked like a snow-covered land). "It's no good going that way," answered the water-carrier, "for I saw him flying east at five o'clock." That was just before the time my message came in, so they took the water-carrier with them and headed east, knowing that there was only one fjord in that direction likely to be ice-free. All through the night the Eskimos had travelled in their kayaks, though the pastor had had difficulty in forcing his motor-boat through the ice-floes.

Rosing said that we were only 35 miles from Angmagssalik (though subsequently I found that the distance was less than 20 in a straight line). I asked him to show me the point on my map, but he could not because the island on which we now stood was unmarked. He therefore drew a pencil sketch to explain where the entrance to Angmagssalik fjord was, and told me to fly well in as the settlement (properly called Tasiusak) is two miles from the open sea. I expected to wait four or five hours for the tide to float me off, so I asked him, if he got back first, to have a smudge fire lit on the highest rocks at the entrance to the fjord. Such a beacon would have made all the difference yesterday when I flew past without seeing anything. I told Rosing how I had almost decided to land in a lake high up, before choosing the fjord, and he recognised from my description a lake that had a settlement of Eskimos on it. Had I landed there, I could have been re-directed and would never have had to spend the night out at all!

Before he left, the pastor said he had brought some bread and tea in the boat, and would I walk over the rocks to the next fjord, or have the Eskimos bring the food to us. I welcomed the exercise, so we all set off for his boat. Several of the Eskimos carried their craft on their heads, but, even so, they obviously found the going easier than I. We went over one snow patch, more rocks, and then came to another stream running through a wide sandy bed. I had seen this from the air. The sand was soft and treacherous which, combined with the swift current and the deepness of the stream, made crossing difficult. As we walked, I talked to Rosing. I asked him if he was a Dane, and he said no. I could not quite make him out, for although he had a fairly dark skin, the shape of his face and his wide-awake intelligence made it impossible for him to be an Eskimo. At last he told me; he had been born on the west coast. "I am what you call 'bastard'," he exclaimed, laughing aloud and showing his white teeth. That explained it, for, of course, on the west coast there are no pure-bred Eskimos left. The population has long since been half-caste, interspersed with Danes, Norwegians, and even Scots from the old whaling days.

On reaching the high rocks at the edge of the fjord, I was able to lie down at full length in the morning sun, which though warm, had not yet succeeded in thawing the ice-skin on the open water. One Eskimo fetched a primus stove from the motor-boat, and soon had it going full blast to heat a tin bowl containing water sprinkled with tea-leaves. Meanwhile the pastor, apologizing for not having brought any seal-meat with him, produced a loaf and some butter. Ravenously I devoured this fare, supplemented by Danish "Kenneckerbred" (a form of rye biscuit). I noticed that several of the Eskimos had collected a little distance away, chattering excitedly. Suddenly, one loosed off his rifle into the water apparently in a fit of child-like exuberation. Another lay down with his rifle supported on a tripod. He was watching for a seal that had been reported. When at length the tea was alleged to be on the boil (tea-leaves still gaily floating on top), all the Eskimos congregated around the bowl. To my surprise they brought with them a small salmon marked by a bullet hole through its head. The Eskimos are reputed to be very poor shots with their 10s. rifles, but this was a display of marksmanship seldom, if ever, equalled in European countries – unless the fellow had hit the wrong salmon! Using our cups as ladles, we each baled out our own share of the tea. It tasted excellent to me.

Before the pastor left, he promised to leave five Eskimos with me. I pointed out that, if there should be a sudden change of weather, I might have to remain another night in the fjord, and if he could spare a canvas or tarpaulin cover from his boat I should be very grateful. However, he had brought a little one-man tent with him, and he arranged for the men to erect it near Robert Bruce. I wrote out two messages to be taken back to the settlement, one to "His Excellency the Governor" (as I then understood the trading manager to be called) thanking him for sending out the rescue party so promptly, and, the other, an urgent wire to my wife, saying that Robert Bruce and I were none the worse for spending the night out. An Eskimo had the blow-lamp going which provided the ignition for the antique 2 h.p. motor of the priest's little boat. Rosing was anxious to take the good news of my finding back without delay, so he set off on his journey to the settlement. His little boat was like a picture as it passed through huge masses of floating ice, the silence being broken only by the gentle phut-phut of its exhaust.

Rosing had written the name of my fjord down in my notebook, as I couldn't possibly remember such a word. It was "Agerderdussog." Now Agerderdussog means in Eskimo "the fjord where they found lead". I was surprised at this because I had seen nothing to suggest the presence of lead-ore. But Rosing hastened to explain that in actual fact nobody, not even the Eskimos themselves, believed that lead could be found in that place. On the contrary, they had discovered that when they had run out of bullets the soapstone near the boulders in my fjord could be pushed down the barrel and was as deadly as lead, if it happened to hit anything. Hence the name "Agerderdussog".

On the march back to Agerderdussog, which must have been nearly two miles away, I tried hard to keep up with my bodyguard, but gave it up, after we had crossed the soft sand. They did not bother about leaving me behind and, once we had gone so far, I did not mind finding my own path between the rocks, though I still felt that I should very much enjoy having someone to talk to. Back at Robert Bruce, I first took out my sponge-bag and brushed my teeth in the stream with a very freshening result. I made all preparations for flying by stowing the covers, replacing the battery, putting the grass-lines back in their box in the port float and pouring in oil. I had brought an extra tin of oil from Reykjavik with me and, when I had emptied its contents into the tank, one of the Eskimos asked, by dumb-show, what I was going to do with the old tin. I had intended to leave it behind in the fjord, but now, seizing the opportunity, I presented the tin to him. His face beamed with delight.

Naturally I was feeling tired and, as it would be several hours before the tide came in, I wanted to have a rest. The men had put the tent up on a piece of mossy ground. Meanwhile they had started to pluck the green leaves of a small rock-plant, resembling dandelion leaves in shape, and eat them with obvious relish. I did not try them myself, thinking that meat for an Eskimo tummy might well be poison for a white man, but went and lay down in the tiny tent. A few moments later, as I reclined with my eyes shut, I became conscious of a peculiar smell. I opened an eye just far enough to see an Eskimo worming his way in; another and another followed until there were six inhabitants piled closely together, in this one-man tent! I was too tired and too grateful to want to turn them out. Even now I dared not resign myself wholeheartedly to sleep, for, if I overslept the tide, we should have to wait a whole day more. At high tide there would be about five minutes, in which I could pull Robert Bruce off, and no more. I knew I could not rely upon the bodyguard to understand such niceties of seaplane-handling, and was therefore continually interrupting my rest to lift the corner of the tent and glance at the slowly rising water. In this manner two or three hours passed until I deemed the time had come for moving down to the beach. There I lay down on the rocks, watching the water creep up the floats. All signs of the night-formed ice had vanished and now a light breeze was blowing into the fjord from the sea. This was most fortunate, because it would have been nearly impossible to have made a safe take-off with the wind from any other direction. Had the wind been off-shore, I estimated that the fjord would have been just too narrow for 180 degrees turn as soon as we were off the water, and it was far too deep for climbing out on a straight course.

As usual, the engine started easily, and I climbed into the cockpit to await the exact moment for pulling off the beach. If I tried to go too early with insufficient water, I should damage the float bottoms and almost certainly bump into semi-submerged boulders. Too late, I should not get off at all. Very gently I opened up the engine, rocking the machine by jumping to and fro in the cockpit. For a moment Robert Bruce hesitated, then, with a little more throttle, glided away. I shut down immediately so as to lessen the impact, if we did strike anything, as we sailed forth on a twisting course to keep clear of the obstacles ahead. Safely we passed beyond the ledge formed on the edge of the fjord by the debris, continually deposited, both by portions of the glacier itself, and also by the erosion of the stream. Now the dark depths below probably extended for hundreds of feet.

Moving as slowly as I could, I taxied right out to the drift ice to observe where the scattered growlers lay. The rising tide had brought more ice into the fjord than there had been when I had landed. On the way back I was able to lay a straight line clear of ice, in order to give the longest possible run outwards. I went towards the Eskimos, steering as close inshore as the boulders would let me. With a final wave I opened the throttle full so as not to waste an inch of ice-free space and swung Robert Bruce into wind. There was not much petrol left, and with this light breeze I expected to be off easily before the thick ice started. Nevertheless we seemed to run a long way and gather speed slowly before, just 60 yards short of a big growler, we soared into the air. It had been an anxious start, I reflected, and I should be glad to reach Angmagssalik where, they said, there was very little ice. Straight over the pack-ice we flew, turning slightly to the right to follow the contour of the steeply slanting coast. No room for engine stoppage here! Soon, as we climbed, I took out the pastor's map from my pocket, to see if I could match it with the coast across the bay. In 10 minutes I had spotted a bonfire on the high rocks, with the Danish flag behind, fluttering in the gentle breeze – the very spot which I had flown past yesterday. I was disappointed to see that the entrance to the fjord was chock-full of ice! As I approached, I still could not discern any signs of life or houses: indeed, it was not until I was well inside, flying low, that I spotted the red spire of a tiny church with several other buildings scattered in the background. I had never imagined that the principal settlement on the east coast could possibly be so minute. Even the half-dozen boats moored in the river estuary, constituting the "inner harbour", were so small that none of them could be bigger than a rowing-boat. However, I was able to land safely.

1999

John Grierson was born in 1909, left Saunderites in 1925 to join the R.A.F., and made a record breaking flight, India – U.K. in 1931. Test pilot, Hawker Siddeley Group in 1938.

As a Wing Commander in WWII. he flew Britain's first jet aircraft, (the Gloster E 28) in 1941. Deputy Director Civil Aviation in British Zone of Germany and worked for the de Havilland Aircraft Co. 1950-62.

Member of the Council of the Royal Geographical Society, and the Committee of the Scott Polar Research Institute 1962-64. Author of several books.

The Story of H.M.S. Hunter

by Commander B.G. Scurfield

Lieutenant-Commander Scurfield was captain of H.M.S. Hunter when she struck a mine off the Spanish coast on May 13th, 1937. The result was that many of the crew were trapped, the oil fuel was 2½ feet deep on the torpedomen's mess desk, there was gas from the batteries in the switchboard room, and the ladder had been blown away. Working in total darkness, Lieutenant-Commander Scurfield saved the lives of five men at the constant risk of his own.

For his gallant action Lieutenant-Commander Scurfield was awarded the Albert Medal, the Peacetime equivalent to the Victoria Cross. Here he writes his own story of the happenings off the coast of Spain in May, 1937.

H.M.S. Hunter, 13th May, 1937

In May, 1937, the Non-Intervention Agreement was still in force with some semblance of rigour. In order to report breaches of this agreement, British men-of-war, usually destroyers, were stationed at certain of the ports under the control of the Spanish government. It was for this reason that the *Hunter* was lying off Almeria on the 13th of May.

We had been there for the best part of a week, keeping a good look-out but seeing very little, and we had not been allowed to anchor. We were due to be relieved on the following day and had promised the Consul to take with us when we left some sixty refugees for Gibraltar. During the forenoon the First Lieutenant had been inshore to make the final arrangements.

The afternoon was warm and sunny; Number One was back; the boat was hoisted and the hands had been piped to make and mend clothes. This meant that most men who were not on watch had settled down for the afternoon to make up for sleep lost during night watches.

At a quarter past two there was a violent explosion under the foremast, a roar of steam, and a jet of oil fuel and water shot up to the level of the bridge. In a very few seconds all the sleepers were on deck. The first person to break the tension was a nineteen-year-old Ordinary Seaman. He had been on duty as a look-out and the blast had catapulted him into the water. He was in no way

HMS Hunter after the accident

injured, but was heard to be enquiring in forcible terms whether we intended to leave him in the water all "night".

By this time the First Lieutenant had the seamen busy turning out and preparing the boats; the Engineer Officer was making sure that all that could be had been done to seal up the ship forward, and others of his department were trying to raise steam in the after boiler. There was time for the Captain to take stock of the situation. The ship was six miles from the town; there was no means of telling anybody what had happened as the wireless was out of action and we could not move. One felt extraordinarily helpless. The next thing was to try and find out the extent of the damage and the number of men who were casualties. The topmast had come down, the motor boat and "skimming dish" were not seaworthy, and going along the upper deck one gradually began to see how really serious the damage was. The foremost boiler-room, which had been steaming at the time, was a mass of twisted wreckage and the deck of the galley (or cookhouse) which was over it had disappeared. The cook, who had been baking at the time, had fallen through and, though he was still alive when got up on deck, he died soon after. His mate miraculously escaped with severe burns and shock. Of the stokehold crew nothing more was ever seen.

Next to the boiler-room, below the upper deck, was the Torpedomen's mess-deck. This and the adjoining Stoker Petty Officers' Mess had been thoroughly wrecked. A number of men had been asleep in them and these had been piled up in one corner dazed and soaked in oil fuel and badly burned. The list the ship had taken up, the lack of light and the all-pervading oil fuel made the job of getting these bodies on to the forecastle a slow one, but in time they and a number of other casualties about the ship were all collected and being dealt with by the Flotilla Medical Officer, who was fortunately borne in the *Hunter*. His job was not simplified by the fact that his Sick Bay had been reduced to a state of chaos.

One of the casualties was a Leading Seaman, who was the approved ship's photographer. His leg was badly broken, but in spite of this he had managed to hoist himself on to a boat out of the way and sat there quietly waiting till someone should have time to give him a hand. His only complaint was that he could not get anybody to go and get his camera for him, and the thought of missing such splendid chances went hard with him. He had to have his leg off later in Gibraltar hospital, poor fellow, but managed somehow or other to get a photograph of the operation!

All this time the ship was listing more and more to starboard. Efforts to raise steam had proved fruitless and orderly arrangements were being made to abandon ship. A fishing boat had been persuaded to come alongside and the wounded had been transferred to her; confidential books and papers had been packed up and put into her, and at length she set off for the shore with part of the ship's company. The rest of the men were in the two whalers and one or two floats.

All possible steps had by this time been taken to keep the ship afloat. She was, however, well down by the bows and the water was just beginning to lap the upper deck on the starboard side. It seemed pointlessly heroic to sit on board when one could watch what the ship was going to do just as well from a boat, and so it was at last decided to abandon ship. The Flotilla football shield, a salver, presented by the builders, and the First Lieutenant's Bedlington terriers, were collected and the officers followed them down to the boat. Dog experts may perhaps be interested to hear that Mona gave birth to a perfectly sound litter of five puppies less than a month later.

The situation now took a new turn. The explosion had been seen by the Captain of the Port and he had collected help, in the shape of the destroyer *Lazaga* and a variety of small craft. After a discussion a mixed party went back on board the *Hunter* and before very long she was in tow, stern first, of three Spanish trawlers. It was at first the intention to beach the ship, but the list was now beginning to improve and eventually she was towed into the harbour and safely berthed at the oil wharf. The Captain of the Port was a tower of strength and could be communicated with in French. Dressed in Sam Browne and dungarees, he kept up a constant flow of objurgation at the trawler skippers, marking periods of greater importance by flourishes of his revolver. He told us that discipline on the government side was very good and showed us that his revolver was fully loaded.

It was a quarter-to-six when we at last got into the harbour, and a muster of the ship's company could be made. Five men were known to have lost their lives and the bodies of three others were recovered later. Eleven wounded men had been taken to the old Spanish battleship *Jaime Primero* and three others to the military hospital. The latter was bad: all and sundry appeared to have the right to visit when they liked, flies were a plague and attendance was very sketchy. Fortunately, our fellows only had to stay there for one night and were taken to Gibraltar by hospital ship next day. The *Jaime Primero*, though very old and looking "chatty" beyond words, had a most efficient medical department, and two men at least owe their lives to the extremely up-to-date treatment given to their burns.

An awning was rigged on the wharf for the survivors; a tot of rum was served out and officers and men made themselves as snug as they could for the night. The difficulty about getting news through had been overcome by the courtesy of the *Jaime Primero*, who had actually sent a first report to Gibraltar before we made contact with her. As a result, the *Hyperion*, of our flotilla, arrived from Malaga just before midnight and she was followed by our leader, *Hardy*, an hour later. They were very welcome. It was not until then that it was possible to send a casualty list to the Admiralty, and after that, reassuring telegrams to our relatives.

Next morning the cruiser *Arethusa* arrived in the bay. A thorough investigation of the damage was not possible, but it was obviously no good leaving the *Hunter* at Almeria, so it was decided to risk the tow to Gibraltar, 157 miles away. This was done by *Arethusa*, *Hardy* having, with fine seamanship, manoeuvred the *Hunter* out of the harbour. The weather was marvellously calm and the passage was made without incident at an average of seven knots. Those of the ship's company and officers who were on board during the trip camped round the mainmast on the upper deck and after seeing the ship after she had been docked down at Gibraltar, were very glad they had done so. There can be little doubt that if there had been any sea the ship would have broken in two, as the two ends of the ship were only held together by some decidedly buckled upper deck plating. The width of the hole at the top was nineteen feet, and at the bilge keel thirty-eight, while the keel itself was distorted for some thirty feet of its run and sheared clean through into the bargain. In addition, the "whip" resulting from the explosion caused a buckling of the entire ship some way further aft – a phenomenon which has greatly exercised the minds of the constructors.

The *Hunter* was patched up temporarily at Gibraltar and was able to steam to Malta on one boiler in August, 1937. She was completely repaired there and was able to take her place in the Second Destroyer Flotilla again in October, 1938, the *Active* having taken her place meanwhile.

The cause of the explosion was undoubtedly a Nationalist mine. A few months later the writer had to pay a call on the Nationalist Commander-in-Chief at Palma. His expression of interest at meeting the Captain of the British destroyer which had nearly been sunk by one of his mines was most gratifying.

1999

Bryan Scurfield was born in 1902, and left Saunderites in 1920, to join the Navy in 1922.

He was awarded the Albert Medal in 1937, and the O.B.E., and a D.S.O. during the war.

He was taken prisoner by the Germans, and unfortunately died of wounds sustained in an air attack on the P.O.W. camp in 1945.

80 Degrees N.

by D.B. Keith

(A Master at Charterhouse in 1939)

North East Land, as the second largest island of the Spitsbergen archipelago is unromantically called, had till 1935 been visited only for short periods, and those infrequently, and thus remained little known. In fact, although Norwegian sealers hunted every summer in the pack ice that encircled it, it was still an enticing conglomeration of dotted lines, question marks and guesswork on every map and chart. It had, however, managed to gain an evil reputation, for not only did it invariably smother any explorer in the vilest weather, but a surprising number of those who had visited it had died upon its shores. In 1935 an expedition of nine men was organised to complete the exploration of the island.

We sailed in July in the *Polar*, our 65 ton boat, and with us went 23 West Greenland dogs, and unknown tons of food and equipment including the timber for a base hut. The pack was far South that year, and the heaving waters of the grey north Atlantic gave place after five days to the sparkling brilliance and calm of the ice. But it was not heavy, and in four days more we had forced a way through to North East Land. Strenuous days of unloading followed; cases of all sizes and weights – one of which contained the Austin 7 engine to generate the current for the wireless

The 'Polar' in the ice

transmitter – had to be man-handled off the boat and up the rocky foreshore. It was the middle of August when the hut was built and our equipment ashore. The *Polar* sailed for Norway, and we were left the only inhabitants of an island about the size of Wales lying less than 600 miles from the Pole.

Three of us left the base soon after the unloading was finished to map the coastline eastwards. In a whaleboat with an outboard motor, carrying food and equipment for six weeks, we gaily started charting enormous stretches of coast each day. But our success was as short lived as the fine weather, for without warning, at the end of September, the pack ice drove down from the north making it impossible to anchor the boat without its being crushed on to the shore. We had to turn for home a fortnight before we should and with the map but half completed. The wind began to rise at once, and soon a series of steep waves broke over the engine. There followed a spell of the wildest activity. I made continuous efforts to restart the motor while we bounced on the tops of the waves, while the others divided their time between pouring our remaining oil on the water as the crests were now breaking into the boat, and rowing furiously to keep us off the ice on to which we were drifting. I failed, but they succeeded; and in the lee of the ice we made the land where we waited ignominiously for three days till the gale stopped. On an expedition there is only one thing that can be relied upon, and it is that no activity will take place exactly as planned. We had learnt the lesson quickly.

We arrived eventually at the base, having had to row as the engine still resolutely refused to function, and immediately two of us were detailed to help the completion of the two ice cap stations. Almost the whole of the interior of North East Land is covered by a permanent sheet of ice, probably several hundred feet thick. One of the main activities of the expedition was to be a study of these ice caps, and for this purpose two stations were established on the ice and equipped, one for the year, and one for six months. Food and gear necessary for the whole time were sledged up before they were inhabited, and, when all was complete, two of us were sent to the main station.

Our tent was twelve feet in diameter and was buried deep in the ice for warmth and as security against the almost continuous gales. We entered the tent by scrambling through a packing case on the surface of the ice about twenty yards from the tent. This was our front door, and it led by a flight of steps cut in the ice to a tunnel some fifteen feet below the surface. We scrambled along this and eventually came up into the tent through a trap door in the middle of the floor. In time the station came to consist of a warren of such tunnels. These led to caverns where our stores were kept, and one was cut downwards into the ice for scientific purposes. At first the digging and use of these tunnels was a claustrophobic nightmare, but it was not long before they became part of our home and as little frightening as the passages at home. Our method of leaving the tent had one disadvantage; for we found that when we stuck our head above the packing case outside, the sudden whirl of driving snow after the calm of the tunnel took our breath away and almost choked us. We did not go outside more than necessary. After October noon was marked merely by a glow in the southern sky, and by mid-November even this had disappeared, it was dark for the twenty-four hours. Meteorological observations were taken three times each day, but except on the rarest occasions it was impossible to do more than gingerly feel one's way from one instrument to the next, as the light of our torches merely lit up a maze of whirling snow and it would have been impossible to find the station again had we once lost our way. It was a strange existence – supremely boring. Continual darkness outside and a small tent, sparsely furnished, to live in; we had our sleeping bags, a few books, a gramophone and a few records, cooking pots, a jumbled mass of unintelligible and usually recalcitrant scientific apparatus. But we had a wireless, a transmitter and receiver, and on the former sent out to the base our weather reports each day whence they were passed to Norway and London. The current for the transmitter was generated by a pedal machine and I spent every evening pedalling hard while the message was being tapped out on the key.

If still, cloudless weather happened to coincide with a full moon, it was virtually as clear as day, and light enough to travel. Shortly before Christmas such a period occurred and a small sledge party arrived from the base bringing someone to take my place for the rest of the winter. We left the station under a dark blue sky studded with a myriad stars. A full moon was shining brilliantly, throwing crisp jet-black shadows of ourselves, the dogs and sledge on the powdery snow. Above all a glorious aurora danced continually across the cloudless sky. We had a light sledge and rode on it thrilled with this opportunity of travelling in the middle of winter darkness. One of us steered by compass while the other took his course from the moon. We were a little mystified by the disagreement which there appeared to be between the two, and when eventually we came to land at the edge of the ice cap we failed to recognise a single landmark and were completely lost. We then discovered that the liquid in the compass was frozen solid. But our luck was in, and we accidentally found the right route again after a delay far shorter than we deserved.

The way down from the ice cap to the base on this, and on every occasion, was an uncontrollable affair. We used a "dead" glacier to descend to the land, but it was very steep and for considerable periods of the year consisted of a slope of highly polished blue ice with hardly a vestige of snow on it to give any sort of foothold. Going down was breathless. The dogs would go as fast as any dog can travel, but the sledge would go faster; and often after passing a ridge in the ice the sledge would continue its descent upside down, tail first or in fact in any but the orthodox position. Sledges and a variety of other equipment were smashed on that slope during the year but we and the dogs always escaped injury.

Winter at the base was soon over. Although it was not possible to do much outside till February there was plenty to be done indoors in preparation for the spring and summer. The two sewing machines whirred continuously, making dog-harnesses, gloves, and blanket trousers and repairing clothing worn out the previous season. The base was also a hive of scientific industry. Research into the behaviour of wireless waves in the ionosphere, work on the aurora, measurements of atmospheric ozone, and weather observations were carried out each day, rigidly controlling all other activities.

For the spring survey programme dumps of food and ammunition were required in various parts of the island, and at the beginning of February we set out with two dog teams to lay the dumps in the south west. The sun had not yet reappeared since the autumn, so it was only possible to travel for a few hours each noon when there was sufficient light in the southern sky. We took with us an experimental light-weight tent. It was not a success. From the first night we realised things would be uncomfortable, but none of us foresaw to what an extent. The tent was single instead of double-walled and as we experienced temperatures down to minus 40°F. the steam from the cooking pot and our breath condensed on the inside of the canvas and formed a thick layer of hoar frost. At every gust of wind the flapping tent shook this load of ice all over us and our sleeping bags. When we were in the bags we thawed, by the heat of our bodies, the ice which fell on us, but during the day's travelling it refroze. This process continued for several days till the sleeping bags were quite useless, they were sodden and then frozen so stiff that they were difficult to unroll; and eventually we had to spend the nights shivering round the primus in a vain attempt to keep warm.

On February 20th the sun appeared above the horizon for the first time since October; we were childishly excited, and every member of the expedition who had a camera, photographed the scene. This marked the beginning of the last stage of our work. The smaller ice cap station was dismantled; the personnel at the other was changed. Preparations for the spring and summer journeys were in full swing.

For the biological work during the coming summer I had planned to work in the "Bay of Islands", which lay some sixty miles to the south of the base. We sledged two big loads of equipment there in March when the dogs were available, and two of us took up our residence there at the end of April. For the final journey we had to man-haul some 800 lbs., and it was unexpectedly complicated by the first thaw of the year. The top layers of the snow began to melt, with the result that for the last week of the journey we dragged our load through ice-cold slush in which we sank to the knees. On one of the earlier journeys the remains of a trapper's tiny hut had been seen on one of the islands in the bay. We dismantled this, hauled it across the ice and re-erected it on the site we had chosen. It became our home for three months.

Our life for the first part of our stay here was enlivened by the presence in the bay of a bear with two very small cubs. They seemed either to ignore us or to consider us harmless and often spent several days playing, resting or hunting within two or three hundred yards of our hut. The mother was apt to abuse our forbearance, and when we had meat lying on the roof would try to stalk up to the hut to steal it. We used to wait till she was close enough for comfort, try somewhat shakily to take a photograph, and then drive her off by rushing out shouting and brandishing rifles. We christened her Emma and we got a lot of fun out of her.

At first we and Emma and a few Ivory Gulls were the only inhabitants of the bay, but in May the birds began to arrive, and the seals would scramble through their holes and lie basking on the ice. By the end of July most of the ice along the coast had broken up. At the beginning of August the whaleboat was able to reach us from the base. The sledge and survey parties returned and gradually the work was finished off. On August 20th the ship arrived from Norway, bringing the first letters we had seen for thirteen months and was soon loaded with as much of our equipment as was in good enough repair to be taken home. The base lay under a grey mass of heavy cloud as we steamed away; it still looked uninviting and vaguely forbidding.

1999

David B. Keith was in Hodgsonites from 1927–1932. He was an Assistant Master at Charterhouse from 1938–1949, though during WWII, he served in the R.A.F.

On leaving Charterhouse he farmed, and is now living in Hampshire.

The World's Long-Distance Record Flight

by Squadron Leader B. K. Burnett, A.F.C.

Sqdn.-Ldr B.K. Burnett was the navigator-pilot of No. 3 aircraft in the R.A.F. World long distance record flight from EGYPT to AUSTRALIA, in 1938.

In 1937 he was R.A.F. squash rackets champion, but was unable to defend his title last year because of the long distance flight.

For the part he played in the flight he was awarded the Air Force Cross, and is now the youngest Squadron Leader in the R.A.F.

Before starting on an account of the actual record flight from Egypt to Australia, I propose to tell you something about the formation of the Unit and all the preparations which led up to the final flight.

The Long Range Development Unit was formed at R.A.F. Station, Upper Heyford, Oxon., on January 1st, 1938, although several members had been working together since the middle of the previous November. It was during the Autumn of 1937 that the Air Ministry decided to form a special unit, the ultimate object of which was to break the existing Long Distance Record by a formation of three aircraft. The record was then held by the Russians, with their 6305.7 mile flight from Moscow, over the North Pole, to the U.S.A.

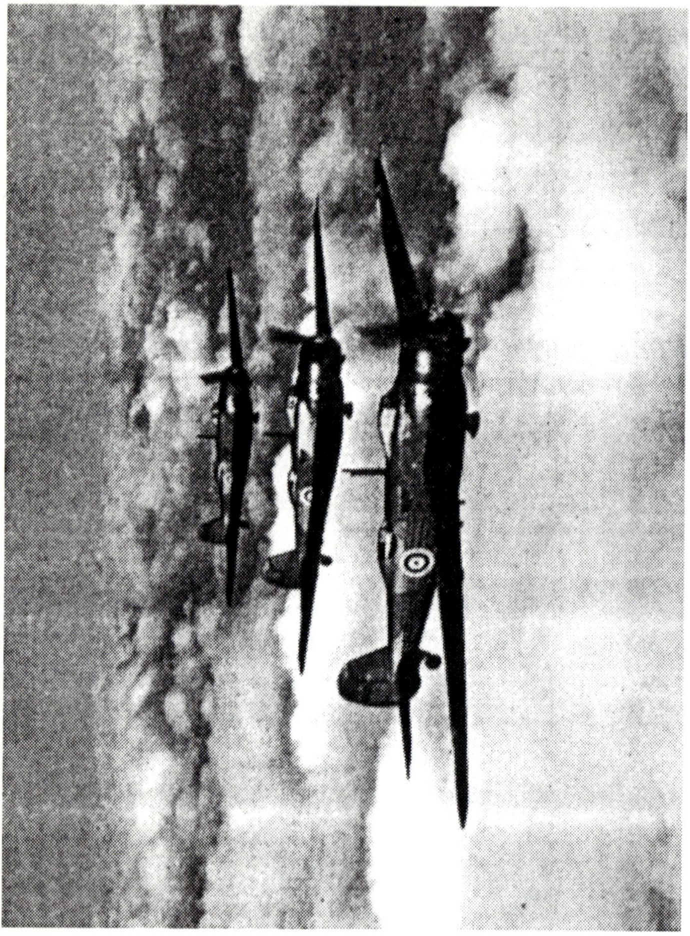

The Three Wellesleys in formation above the clouds

The equipment of the Unit was to be five Vickers Wellesley single engined bombers of the standard type, with which several squadrons of the R.A.F. had already been equipped. Modifications, of course, were to be made, as necessary. Four crews, consisting of chief pilot, navigator, and wireless operator (both the latter being also pilots), were selected and the Unit was placed under the command of Wing Commander O.R. Gayford, D.F.C., A.F.C., who, together with Flight Lieutenant G.E. Nicholetts, A.F.C., had previously held the World's Long Distance Record for the R.A.F. with their flight from Cranwell, Lincs., to Walvis Bay, S. Africa, a distance of about 5,300 miles. The crews were all young – between the ages of 25 and 31, and were all specialists in their different jobs.

The route finally chosen for the record attempt was the Great Circle Route from Ismailia, Egypt to Darwin, Australia, though this was slightly modified, as it was found that it involved sea crossings of over 1,000 miles across the Arabian Sea, and of over 1,300 miles across the Bay of Bengal. The modification consisted of dividing up the route into three Great Circles, the first from Ismailia to Jask, the second from Jask to Port Blair in the Andaman Islands, and the third from Blair to Darwin. By doing this the crossing of the Bay of Bengal was reduced to two crossings of 800 and 450 miles, and the actual increase in distance was only two or three miles. I should, perhaps, point out here that for Record purposes, it is the Great Circle distance that counts. i.e. the shortest distance between the two places on the earth's surface. Even on this route nearly 60 per cent. or 4,000 miles was over the sea.

As a safety precaution the Air Ministry and the Admiralty made arrangements to provide:

A Persian Gulf Sloop in the Arabian Sea.
A Royal Indian Marine Sloop in the Bay of Bengal.
A Royal Australian Navy Sloop in the Timor Sea.

The R.A.F.A. Aquarius in the South China Sea.
Flying Boats from Singapore in the Andaman Islands and at Kuching in Sarawak.

The fact that none of these were seen during the flight, owing to the cloud below, did not detract from their value, and we were in wireless communication with them all.

The International 1/1,000,000 Series of Maps were obtained to cover the whole route as far as the land was concerned and various Admiralty charts of scales varying from about 15 statute miles to 1 inch to about 45 statute miles to 1 inch to cover the areas over the sea. These were joined together in strips and made up into four rolls.

By about the middle of April, all five aircraft had been delivered to the Unit, suitably modified. The engine was a Bristol Pegasus XXII, which developed a little over 1,000 h.p. for take-off at 2,600 r.p.m., and would run economically at a very low power output at 1,500 r.p.m. A Rotol constant speed airscrew and an automatic pilot were fitted. The tankage was increased from about 400 galls. to 1,260 galls., and the petrol was carried in the wings of the aircraft. The interior lay-out was also slightly altered and added to – stowages for food, drink, navigational equipment, etc., having to be fixed in positions that restricted the available space as little as possible.

Changing seats when taking over piloting was always a rather clumsy manoeuvre in these aircraft owing to the narrow fuselage. The pilot's seat had to be let down from behind, and the pilot crawled out backwards. Then the relief pilot scrambled in, and the seat was returned and locked in position. With practice this was carried out quite quickly and easily.

Jettison valves were fitted so that the petrol could be jettisoned, and in the event of a forced landing in the sea, it was calculated that the aircraft would float indefinitely in a level attitude, providing, of course, that she did not break up, but fortunately this was never put to the test.

Flotation jackets were provided, but parachutes were discarded, as we did not expect the aircraft to break up or collide in the air, neither did we expect ice formation. Also, as the larger part of the route lay over the sea, parachutes would not have been of much use.

It was planned that the height at which we should fly should be 10,000 feet or above, the engines being designed to run most economically at this height. Actually, it was really a case of the higher the better, but the strain of flying for a long time much above 10,000 or 12,000 feet would have been rather too much, as it was not intended to carry oxygen.

The speeds at which we should fly were all worked out beforehand by the makers. At the start the speed was to be about 175 m.p.h. True, falling as the load decreased to about 130 m.p.h., at the end. This may seem odd, as you would think that speed would be increased as the load was lessened. The reason is that an aeroplane has one altitude where the lift-drag ratio is the highest, and the idea was that the Wellesley should be flown in this altitude, and the speed should be varied to obtain the requisite amount of lift according to the load. In practice, full instructions were given as to what revs. and what boost the engine should run at, and it was hoped that the speed would be as forecast. If the speed was down, the throttle was opened a little to increase the speed sufficiently. On the Record flight one of the aircraft could not get the required speed at the start without going into rich mixture, whereas the leader's aeroplane seemed to do slightly better than the makers had hoped. Automatic carburettors were fitted to the engines and the constant speed airscrews made it possible to open the throttle and increase the boost, and therefore the power output, without increasing the revs.

Just as the best training for a particular game is constant practice at that game, so the best training for long distance flights is also practice, and we gradually acclimatised ourselves to flying for extended periods at 10,000 feet or above. Five hour flights were followed by 12-hour flights round the British Isles, and later by 16 hours and 30-hour flights to Egypt via the Persian Gulf and from Egypt to England.

Apart from this, there was plenty to be done with automatic pilot tests, consumption tests, and general aircraft performance tests, as the aircraft were delivered direct to us, and all the tests were carried out by the Unit. Each crew was allotted their particular aircraft and carried out the tests on it. By the end of May all the tests were completed, and permission was obtained to carry out an extended trial flight of nearly 4,500 miles, at the beginning of July. The route was to be Cranwell (Lincs.) – Ismailia (Egypt) – Basra – down the Persian Gulf for about 200 miles and back to Ismailia. All four aircraft left Cranwell at dawn on July 7th and flew over Holland, Belgium, Germany, Austria, Italy, Jugo-Slavia, Albania, Greece, and then a few Italian islands and across nearly 400 miles of the Mediterranean. Ismailia was reached soon after dark, and by daybreak the next day we were somewhere South of Basra. The aircraft had become separated after four or five hours in the air, as we were all flying according to the revs. and boost laid down for each particular engine, so that the full range of the aircraft could be calculated after the flight. All four aircraft had landed by local noon July 8th, at Ismailia, after a flight of about 31 hours.

After a stay of nearly a fortnight in Egypt, the Unit flew back to Upper Heyford, ending up in formation after a 16-hour flight on July 21st. Breakfast in Egypt and dinner in Oxford.

After these trial flights the work of overhauling the aircraft and fitting new engines began, and again there were one or two modifications to be carried out, based on experience gained on the trial flights. The intention now was to leave for Egypt at the end of September, so that the actual start might be made from Ismailia during the full moon period at the beginning of October. Unfortunately, owing to the international situation at that time, the flight was postponed indefinitely, and it was not till a month later that we were allowed to proceed to Egypt. This time all five aeroplanes were taken in case spares were needed at the last moment, and we flew out in formation in two hops, spending a night at Malta en route.

We arrived at Ismailia on the 26th October, and the next ten days or so were spent mostly on the ground, putting the final touches to everything. It was finally decided that three aircraft should take off for Australia towards the end of the first week in November. Weather reports for the whole route were received every evening at Ismailia, and after consultation with the Met. Officer on the evening of November 4th, the three aircraft were wheeled out on to the runway and filled up with petrol preparatory to leaving at dawn the next day. As a matter of fact, in order to save unnecessary strain on the undercarriages, the aircraft were not completely filled up until a short while before time of departure.

I am afraid I have taken up a lot of time and space describing the preparations before the flight. It was, however, during these preparations that the real work was done which made the actual Record Flight possible.

At 0355 hours G.M.T. on Saturday, November 5th, as soon as it was light enough to see the runway, the three aircraft took off one after the other from Ismailia, turned slowly on to the course 096 degrees T., and started to climb up gradually. As Squadron Leader Kellett has often said since: "The Record Flight could be described in a few simple words: there was really nothing to see and really nothing to go wrong." Nothing to see, due to the nature of the route chosen, and nothing to go wrong, such was the unbounded confidence we had in our aircraft and engines that this was truly how we felt. However, there are a few points which might be of interest.

The take-off was possibly a little problematical, so that we all felt rather more at ease once we were airborne. The aircraft handled very well under the fully loaded conditions, and the climb to 10,000 feet was done in about 32 minutes, with the exception of No. 3 aircraft which was delayed temporarily, having trouble retracting the undercarriage.

The first part of the route lay across Arabia, and those of you who have never been out in those parts may rest assured that they have not missed anything, as there is nothing to see but sand. We reached the Persian Gulf after six hours, having covered about 1,000 miles at an average ground speed of approximately 170 m.p.h.

The weather had been cloudy and bumpy for most of this time, but going down the Persian Gulf conditions were good with the sky clear and excellent visibility. Darkness fell as we reached a point on the Persian Coast near Jask, and four hours later the Indian Coast was picked up by the light of the moon, 14 hours after the start of the flight. India was crossed by night, clouds obscuring the ground the entire way. It was a glorious night above the clouds, with the full moon, and navigation was carried out by sextant star sights. Although we flew right across India we cannot say we saw much of it. Just as dawn broke we reached the East Coast of India after some 20 hours, nearly, 3,300 miles having been covered. We then set off on the crossing of the Bay of Bengal. All instruments were reading so steadily that the needles might have been fixed in one position. We started encountering heavy cumulous clouds after about an hour, and for the next four or five hours we were in and out of thunder clouds and rainstorms. Attempts were made to avoid these to start with, but as this made navigation rather difficult, a steady course was maintained.

The Andaman Islands were sighted through a break in the clouds – a welcome sight – some six hours after leaving India, and a course was set for Malaya. The weather improved a bit here, and we picked up the Malayan Coast under good conditions. We crossed the Malay Peninsula, and clouds began to form up just as night fell. We had then covered some 5,000 miles. From then until dawn the weather deteriorated and nothing was seen of Borneo, as we were in heavy clouds, thunderstorms, lightning and rain, during this time.

We had gradually become separated as the flight progressed, as it was essential for each aircraft to maintain its set engine conditions at all times, both for minimum consumption and for maximum performance, and for these particular conditions the performance of each aircraft varied slightly. Although not in formation, all three aircraft were in constant touch with each other by wireless (R/T). When dawn came at the end of the second night after having flown blind for about six hours, we were able to see below through broken clouds, and check up on our position. At that time we were able to work out fairly accurately the possibility of reaching Darwin. It was then found that No. 1 Aircraft was quite confident, No. 2 was doubtful, and No. 3 was satisfied, so a rendezvous was arranged at a place called Lomblen Island in the Dutch East Indies, so that we could do the last lap together. A further check up on the fuel question showed that No. 2 Aircraft might be unable to make a landfall in Australia with any margin of safety. The alternative was to land. A decision was made and it landed at Koepang: an unenviable position to be in when so close to its destination. However, it was unquestionably the right decision, and the fact that the landing was made, the aircraft refuelled, and flown straight on to Darwin within a few hours, reflects credit on the crew concerned. Nos. 1 and 3 Aircraft carried on across the Timor, No. 1 slowing down, and No. 3 increasing sped so that they met in the air over the Timor Sea and flew the last hour on to Darwin in formation, arriving at 0400 hours G.M.T., or 1300 hours local time, on November 7th.

A few words to end up with on the equipment and personnel side of the flight. Thanks to the Automatic Pilot which, apart from one or two minor and rectifiable troubles, behaved extremely well, the flight was no strain on the personnel. (This is borne out by the programme for the rest of the day in Darwin. A late lunch, followed later by a cocktail party, Guest night dinner in the Staff Corps Mess and a Victoria League Dance).

Sleep, under the conditions inside the aircraft was hardly possible, but the fact that one changed over duties at certain periods gave the necessary relief. It was found rather trying flying into the sun all day, and the pilot's cockpit was unpleasantly warm at times. Eye soreness was the only physical discomfort encountered. Navigation throughout the flight was most satisfactory, using the sextant for sun and star observations, and D/F stations along the route for occasional checks. Only about a quarter of the food carried was consumed, probably owing to restricted movement. The favourite food was fresh fruit and the favourite drink iced water. Everyone managed to shave and wash before arrival.

After landing at Darwin No. 1 Aircraft still had 44 gallons of petrol left, and No. 3, 17 gallons – enough for another 2½ and 1 hours' flying time, respectively. The average ground speed throughout the flight was approximately 150 m.p.h., there being an average head wind of about 10 m.p.h. The Great Circle Distance between Ismailia and Darwin for record purposes is 7158.653 statute miles and the time taken was 48 hours 05 minutes.

The crews were as follows:–

No. 1 Aircraft:

Squadron Leader R. Kellett, Pilot.
F/Lieut. R.J. Gething, Navigator-Pilot.
Pilot Officer M.L. Galne, W/Opr.-Pilot.

No. 2 Aircraft:

F/Lieut. H.A.V. Hogan, Pilot.
F/Lieut. R.G. Musson, Navigator-Pilot
F/Sergt. T.D. Dixon, W/Opr.-Pilot.

No. 3 Aircraft:

F/Lieut. A.N. Combe, Pilot
F/Lieut. B.K. Burnett, Navigator-Pilot
Sergt. H.B. Gray, W/Opr.-Pilot

No. 2 Aircraft held the World's Non-Stop Straight Line Distance Record for their flight Ismailia (Egypt) – Koepang (Timor) 6,658.452 miles for a few hours until No. 1 and No. 3 landed at Darwin, having covered 7,158 miles. Thus, the Russian Record was beaten by all three aircraft – by some 350 miles by No. 2, and some 850 miles, by both Nos. 1 and 3 Aircraft.

The crews who took part in this flight were just the lucky ones chosen to sit there, and we hoped that the success achieved by the aircraft was in itself sufficient reward for the maintenance personnel of the Long Range Development Unit. During the months of training and practice prior to the commencement of the actual flight, the men had worked long and odd hours, very often all night, so that the planes should be ready in the morning. The credit for the flight must go to those who designed and produced the aircraft and engines capable of this performance – Messrs. Vickers Armstrong and The Bristol Aeroplane Company.

Records such as this are, of course, only made to be broken, and it will probably not be long before this distance of 7,158 statute miles is also exceeded. However, it might be remembered that this flight was carried out not by one specially designed aeroplane, but by three slightly modified aeroplanes of standard type in the Royal Air Force to-day.

1999

Air Chief Marshal Sir Brian Burnett was born in 1913. He left Saunderites in 1930 to go up to Oxford, from where he joined the R.A.F. In WWII, he was in Bomber and Flying Training Commands.

He was A.D.C. to Queen Elizabeth II 1953–57, and Air Secretary, Ministry of Defence 1967–70, C-in-C Far East Command, Singapore 1970, and retired in 1972.

He was the R.A.F. lawn tennis champion in 1937 and 1939, R.A.F. squash rackets champion 1937, 1946, 1949, 1950–1.

Chairman of All England Lawn Tennis Club in 1974, President Squash Rackets Association 1972–75, President O.C. Club 1968.

A Memory of Charterhouse

by C. Aubrey Smith

You ask me, Mr. Editor, for a word from the Stage or the Cinema? Well, I can, perhaps, trace the root of all my theatrical experiences to a performance at Charterhouse.

We were doing a Pantomime – Ali Baba; and being small enough, then, to be squeezed into one of the "jars", I was cast for one of the 40 Thieves.

The piercing scream, which issued from that jar, was apparently far-reaching enough to get me a "part" in the next production.

That was the first rung on the ladder, which brought me to the glare of publicity, which emanates from Hollywood. I don't mean this as a slur on Hollywood at all, for Hollywood itself is not nearly as bad as it often makes itself appear.

I wonder, do the boys still play "punt-about" with tennis balls in the quad behind Gownboys? We used to in my time, and I remember one occasion when an opportunity occurred to recover some of those which had lodged on the roof of what were then the "Stinks" class-rooms. I found 42 lawn tennis balls up there – a very fortune.

However, I would not advise any youngster to attempt it, even if an opportunity did occur, because it involved extra drill for me for the rest of the term.

1999

He was born in 1863 and left Charterhouse in 1881, to go up to Cambridge. He was in the Cambridge Cricket XI from 1882–85, and played for Sussex from 1882–96. He also played for the English XI to South Africa in 1888–89.

He became an actor and theatrical manager, and was awarded the C.B.E. in 1938, and knighted in 1944.

He died at Beverley Hills, California, in 1948.

What German Youth is Being Taught

by G. A. Rowan-Robinson

(A Master at Charterhouse in 1939)

It has been frequently said that the best way to get to understand a nation's mentality is to study what is being taught in the schools of that country. This may not always be the case, but it is unquestionably true of Germany to-day; for nowhere can one obtain a better picture of National Socialism than in the schools.

The aim of education in Germany to-day is first and foremost, and to the exclusion of almost all else, to make the rising generation loyal and whole-hearted National Socialists. Education has, in fact, become merely an instrument – perhaps the most important – of propaganda for the government. The purpose of this propaganda is to stultify the critical faculty and discourage the unprejudiced presentation of facts, and instead to arouse the emotions. People must cease to *think*; they must *feel*: they must experience the greatness of National Socialism through their emotions.

This propaganda penetrates everywhere. There is hardly such a thing left in Germany to-day as a private school. The few that have managed to survive are kept under very strict supervision and have to conform in every way with the demands of the government. Moreover, in all schools every subject in the curriculum is taught with the sole idea of making the children better Nazis. No subject has for them, then, any intrinsic value at all. Art for Art's sake is a decadent doctrine. Latin, for instance, has little value for them except as a means of finding out what Caesar or Tacitus thought about the Germans. If, however, either of these august authorities should venture a slightly critical remark about the habits or character of these early Germans, the passage is either violently annotated or omitted altogether. The assertion which Tacitus makes, for example, that their ancestors were heavy drinkers is considered a scandalous piece of libel.

The intellectual level of a school may often be gauged fairly accurately from a study of the contents of the school library. In 1937 a decree was published in Germany ordering all schools to clear out their libraries and build them up afresh; and at the same time a list of books, which was to form the basis of every library, was given, and a catalogue of other books recommended. There is no space to enumerate the books, but the picture one gets from them is, to say the least, appalling. They are almost all devoted to depicting the history of Germany as a story of war and race. With the exception of "Robinson Crusoe" and some of the works of Homer and Plato (the latter being very popular because of the anti-democratic tendency of "The State") there is an almost entire absence of foreign literature. Completely ignorant of Christian and European culture, the young are to be brought up in a narrow National Socialist and racial "Weltanschauung" to a national arrogance which claims world domination as its right, and knows no other way of preparing for it or attaining it than through efficiency in arms and military achievement.

A book appeared a short time ago, written by a director of a school in Berlin on the teaching of history in schools. It opens with the following quotation from Reinhold Schneider's "Die Hohenzollern":–

"It is the highest function of history to increase not knowledge but will; not to unveil the past, but to awaken aims and the strength to strive after them."

The author then states that the approach to history must be through the emotions, and points out how the picture that a nation forms of its past is continually changing as the nation changes. "We find in National Socialism how a victorious political movement reveals a new aspect of history. It deliberately establishes the link with the past and changes the value of historical periods and personages." The figure of Charlemagne, for instance, may no longer be honoured. Although he may have been great in many respects, he did Germany a lot of harm, so that the children, who formerly learnt of him as Charles the Great, must cease to refer to him as "the Great", but simply as the King or Emperor Charles.

The league of National Socialist Teachers recently published a pamphlet on Mathematical instruction, entitled "Problems of Commercial Mathematics, dealing with National Socialist reconstruction, for use in the 7th and 8th classes." The following are some of the headings in the pamphlet: "Aviation is necessary", "Our Nation must not die", "Blood and Soil", and so on. And this is the type of problem set, for example, in the section "Aviation is necessary":

"A squadron of 46 bombers drops incendiary bombs on a hostile city. Every machine carries 500 bombs of 1½ pounds each. Calculate the total weight of bomb freight. How many fires will be caused if a third of the bombs hit their objectives and if only 20 per cent. of these cause fires?"

Art and music have also become shackled to politics. Children are shown how national characteristics reveal themselves in sculpture and painting. They are told that the Germanic genius has in the past been hampered by having to adhere to Christian or international formulae. It has even been vigorously asserted that the text of the Gospel lies like a dead weight on the music of the St. Matthew Passion, and that Bach would have created something far greater if his genius could have found outlet in more national channels.

Religion even has become a matter of politics. It has ceased to be denominational within the schools. It is taught now as a school subject with the object of providing a National Socialist Faith, based largely on the works and utterances of Alfred Rosenberg, whose "Myth of the 19th Century" is regarded as the classic work on the subject. The children are taught to take every opportunity they can to ridicule the Church. They are taught not so much to renounce Christianity as to interpret it in a new fashion. In the words of Herr Kerrl, Minister for Church affairs:

"Christ must be taught according to the laws of our time and circumstances. The content of Christ's teaching must be altered. There has now arisen a new authority as to what Christ and Christianity really are. This new authority is Adolf Hitler."

"It is not Christianity", writes Rosenberg "that has brought us civilisation. What lasting values there are in Christianity are owed to the German character."

In order, as it were, to add a little artistic verisimilitude to these new doctrines, the schools have evolved new kinds of services. There is, for example, the *Morgenfeier*, which is equivalent to Morning Chapel. This takes place generally in the school hall, which in some cases is a converted chapel, now swathed in blood-red swastika banners. The service usually consists of a series of recitals of short patriotic poems or stirring events from the history of National Socialism, interspersed with music of a highly martial and patriotic flavour. Then there is the *Sonnenwendfeier*, which takes place at the summer and winter solstices. On this occasion the whole school assembles on a neighbouring hill round a huge bonfire. The service has been carefully rehearsed beforehand. Out of the ranks of boys lined up in military formations single voices are raised intoning some articles of the new faith or extracts from one of Adolf Hitler's speeches. Then at a given signal the whole school bursts out into one of their songs. Finally, the headmaster gives an address in which he stresses the significance of the ceremony, a thanksgiving for God's eternal gift of the Sun, and points out how they are acting in the same way as their Forefathers did many centuries ago.

The most important subject in the curriculum is, after German, biology, which has now become a compulsory subject for all over 10. For under the heading of biology the principles of the new German philosophy of Race or Blood are expounded, which forms the basis of their whole *Weltanschauung* It is worth while examining these principles for a moment and seeing what they really mean.

The Germans claim that in 100 years time, when the historian sits down to write about the present age, he will point out that the outstanding result of National Socialism was a return to the fundamental laws of life. By this is meant, not a romantic "Back to Nature" movement of a Rousseau, but a revival of respect for the laws of natural life. What it amounts to briefly is that they are trying to reduce man to the level of animals and even of plants. His development is regarded in exactly the same way as the growth of, let us say, a geranium. Just as there are certain biological laws governing the growth of a geranium, so there are corresponding biological laws which control the growth of man. These laws, in the German view, govern not only the growth of his body, but also that of his mind and character.

The world is divided up into a number of different racial stocks, just as the world of plants is divided into a number of species. And as the characteristics of a geranium differ from those of a cabbage, so the characteristics of the various races differ from one another. Moreover, they are not all of equal value. As the lily of the valley is considered to be superior to the chickweed, in the same way the Aryan race is in their view superior to all other races. This Aryan race has, apparently, all the characteristics of greatness, the monopoly of all the good qualities. It is even assumed that if a man is born a pure Aryan, he will have not only certain physical characteristics, but certain moral and mental ones also, and will react to given circumstances in a certain way. As an illustration:

> A master in a well-known Berlin school was taking a class in which there were twenty-nine little Aryans and one little Jew. The master had just painted a vivid word picture of a sunrise, and he now asked his audience what impression this picture made on them, what their reactions to it were. What did it make them feel? The twenty-nine little Aryans sat glumly silent. Only the little Jew held up his hand. So finally the master was forced to turn to him. The Jew said that it made him feel the littleness of men and the greatness of the Universe, and proceeded to enlarge on these lines. The master looked puzzled and annoyed. Finally he said: "I can't understand it at all. That is precisely what the twenty-nine others of you are meant to feel. It is quite inconceivable that a non-Aryan should experience such sentiments."

This Aryan race, then, and more particularly the Nordic race, which is a part of it, has certain qualities which, it is felt, it is essential to preserve. Germans in the past have been prevented by such shackles as Christianity, party politics and class barriers from developing these qualities freely. Now the State, by removing these shackles, has enabled the individual for the first time to develop along those lines which are decreed by biological laws and which are therefore natural to him. In fact, the theory is that the individual has for the first time been enabled to win a genuine freedom.

The flaws in such a theory are too obvious to need enumerating; nevertheless the fact cannot be denied that at present the youth of Germany, certainly those up to eighteen or nineteen, are happy under the treatment they are receiving. For one thing, the average German sets a much higher value on sheer efficiency than does the Englishman, and he is prepared to sacrifice personal comforts and personal liberty so that the full efficiency of the machine of which he is a cog, may be achieved. Moreover the youth of Germany have such faith in their Leader and in the regime, that they genuinely do feel that what they are ordered to do is what they themselves would choose to do if the decision were left in their hands. How long such enthusiasm will last is another matter. Up till now it has been a comparatively easy task to maintain it at a high pitch, as Hitler's foreign policy has been so eminently successful. The young Teuton's heart burns with a patriotic fervour when he hears the greatness of Adolf Hitler contrasted with the corruption of Communism and the decadence of the Democracies. Hitler has unquestionably discovered the means of working up mass enthusiasm, but the price he will eventually have to pay for it may well prove to be a high one. For, may it not be that all this propaganda, which stirs up the enthusiasm, is working upon the German mentality in the same way as a stimulating drug works upon the nervous system? It is continually bolstering up the body and giving it the appearance of life and energy, while in reality it is all the time wearing it out, and the doses have to be administered in ever-increasing quantities.

1999

Mr G. Anthony Rowan-Robinson, M.B.E. came to Charterhouse, as a Master, in 1935.

He was the Housemaster of Verites from 1950 to 1965, and was Second Master of the School from 1966–1970, when he retired.

He died in 1989.

Whither Germany?

by A. W. Tressler

(A Master at Charterhouse in 1939)

Spectacular triumphs such as the German Government has achieved in the foreign field are apt to foster the belief that the National-Socialist State is going from strength to strength. Nevertheless, visitors to Germany who have open eyes and ears, are tempted to think that the climax has been reached. They ask themselves whether the imposing edifice that dominates the European stage is more than a back-curtain, designed and lighted with such skill that the very actors believe in its solidity. But whereas in the imaginary world of the theatre it is only the spectators who have to be convinced, the drama of politics demands from the actors themselves a whole-hearted belief in the genuineness of the world in which they play their part. Political loyalties cannot outlast the faith from which they have sprung. The more extravagant the hopes, the stronger will be the reaction, and the catastrophe (brought by disillusionment) may be nearer than we think.

When Germany hailed Hitler as her Saviour, she was a pariah among the nations, her people were disunited, her factories were idle, nearly seven millions were unemployed. Her frontiers were undefended, her fighting forces were restricted, she was not even mistress in her own house. Today she is again a first-class power, there are work, wages, and food for all, distressed areas have vanished from the land. Instead of being threatened by others, it is she who threatens, and behind her Government stands an apparently united people.

This miraculous transformation is the work of one man, and whatever they may think of his methods, Germans in general accept with gratitude the material results of his policy. And they have much to be grateful for. It is foolish and mischievous to disparage everything that the National-Socialist State has accomplished. The Social services of Germany are in their scope and efficiency a model to the world, and these services, it must be remembered, are not confined to active members of the "party": they are open to all, provided the recipient is an Aryan. In particular, the care for the physical development of German children is quite wholly admirable. The alleged food shortage which is so often reported in our newspapers is a myth. It is often impossible to buy exactly what one would like, but there is enough to eat, and there is no difficulty in procuring wholesome and adequate meals.

A regulated diet, however, is more tolerable for the body than for the mind, and a controlled press, a censored literary output, a propagandist wireless service and the inflammatory speeches of the Fuehrer and his satellites, are not calculated to produce healthy minds and souls. The political resurrection of Germany has been bought at a very big price. In the Nazi State we search in vain for the higher spiritual values and it is the soulless resurrection of a material body bereft of personality and functioning like a robot. The professedly benevolent tyrants who control it have risen to power by fostering and exploiting a common hate, and that is in the last resort a disruption, not a binding force. It is a poison that slowly permeates the system, warping the mind and leading to persecution-mania. The man who hates sufficiently long and sufficiently well will end by committing murder or suicide, and the German people is drifting into this condition. The Nazi is taught to love his neighbour and hate his enemy – a doctrine borrowed without acknowledgement from the Old Testament – but as he recognises as his neighbour none but members of his own race, amongst all of these, there is obviously more scope for hate than for love. And when he loves, he loves not so much persons as personified abstractions for whose sake he is prepared to sacrifice not only his fellow men but himself. They become objects of mystical worship and fanatical enthusiasm. One is prompted to think that the full-blooded Nazi of today aims less at material prosperity than at proving to the world that the German as such is a superman. His superiority must be shown by Victory. *Sieg Heil! Sieg Heil! Sieg Heil!* But victory is impossible without material resources, and in spite of the recent annexations the material resources are becoming increasingly inadequate. The internal debt has risen alarmingly, and though there is little or no unemployment, the persons who are employed directly or indirectly in work of national defence are not engaged in productive labour. The unemployment problem is therefore not solved, and the amount of goods for sale abroad in exchange for much needed war materials is not increased. Meantime wages are low and the cost of living high, mainly because the self-imposed desire for economic independence entails the use of expensive substitutes for goods that could either be more cheaply imported or more cheaply manufactured at home if the proper raw materials were available. Artificial wool and rubber are very costly. Oil and many basic metals have still to be imported. In the event of war they would be difficult to obtain in sufficient quantities to meet the needs of the fighting forces. And owing to want of replacements the German railways are very short of goods wagons and locomotives.

The nightmare of inflation is probably the main cause to which we can attribute the general acceptance of a system that inflicts such inconvenience and demands such sacrifices. It is felt that at all costs there must be no recurrence of the catastrophe of 1923. When the French troops occupied the Ruhr, the mark fell to the rate of 150,000 millions to the pound. New and bigger notes were printed day and night. As soon as they were put into circulation they had to be converted into food, for within a few hours their purchasing power was halved. The fruits of years of thrift were destroyed. It was difficult to pay for the barest necessaries of life. Thousands starved to death, unemployment was rampant. But until the mark was re-stabilised old debts and mortgages could be paid off at the face value of the currency notes, and valuable property could be acquired for nothing. For these disasters the blame is officially laid on the Jews and the liberal statesmen, who were then at the head of the State, and this belief, whether justified or not – and it must be admitted that a large number of Jews turned the occasion to profit – is the basis of the racial and political persecutions which humane and intelligent Germans deplore. Much of the injustice and cruelty of Nazism is known in Germany, but much more is not, and if the facts were published they would be disbelieved. The things that happen in the Columbia House in Berlin and in the Buchanwald Camp, near Wirman, are indeed scarcely credible, yet they are well authenticated. Decent Germans accept Hitlerism and its attendant restrictions and cruelties because they know that any revolutionary change – and no other change is possible – will bring with it economic ruin. In return for a guaranteed subsistence, often out of regard for their dependants, they sacrifice the present in the hope of a better future. The belief that Economic prison will bring better conditions has buoyed them up.

The presumed necessity for economic freedom, by which is meant entire economic independence, is the ground on which Germany's claims to Colonies and European expansion are based. But the question is being increasingly asked whether such independence is attainable and whether in striving to attain it the country is not being ruined. The expansion of Germany in Central

Europe has brought no permanent economic benefit. The newly annexed States are being systematically plundered, but the economic policy of the new Germany calls for more and still more. Her hunger is insatiable. What she cannot steal she proposes to get by trade agreements. But there are limits to dumping and the capacity and willingness of the "backward" States of South-Eastern Europe to absorb German goods for which they have little use, and to adopt a form of civilisation which is alien to their nature. Germany's exports are diminishing at a time when their expansion is a condition of her economic vitality. This fact is admitted by the Government, but for obvious reasons is not emphasized except when special circumstances demand it. A fact, however, which must obtrude itself on every German is that the severe economy which is enforced on private individuals is not practised by the Government and its officials. There are innumerable flag-days for all kinds of civil purposes, yet money is being squandered on unnecessary public buildings and patriotic displays. The mobilisation of last September cost millions of pounds; it may, however, be argued that Bohemia and Moravia were cheap at the price. But even the blindest patriot must realise that the deliberate wrecking of Jewish houses and Jewish businesses has impoverished the country without any compensatory advantage to the exact extent of the value of the property destroyed. It is assessed at £80,000,000. The repercussions of this savagery may yet prove embarrassing: it was not only a crime, but a blunder: it has made converts from – not to – Nazism from considerations of expediency as well as of humanity.

Much sympathy is felt with the pitiful plight of the Jews, but any open manifestation would defeat its own end; the party machine is too strong. It would be impossible to convince a public meeting or to move a resolution protesting against their treatment. Even to show private charity requires courage. Nevertheless, high minded individuals have succeeded not indeed in preventing excesses, for they are unpreventable, but in mitigating their consequences. The orgy of destruction last November has evoked disgust and scepticism. In so far as he has not become corrupted by an ideological fanaticism which makes a virtue of ruthlessness the German is by nature, frugal and kindly. The cruelty of the November pogroms is as abhorrent to him as their wastefulness. It is well to remember that many Jewish families deprived of the right to buy food for themselves, had their shopping done for them by Gentiles, though it was known that detection might involve severe penalties. In Cologne, at any rate, there was nothing spontaneous in the so-called anti-Jewish riots. They were the work of S.A. men, acting under orders. The police were forbidden to interfere, and the public stood by, dazed and dumbfounded.

To criticize the policy of the Government, even in private, is dangerous, in a State where spies abound and the mere fact of not buying the *Volkischer Beobachter* is taken for a proof of disloyalty. But there are occasions when criticism takes an indirect and much appreciated form, especially on occasions such as the carnival at Cologne, where there is a traditional licence of speech, and at places of entertainment visited, sallies against the government are received with applause. Here are some. "Who are the most distinguished inventors of today?" – "Hitler, Goering and Goebbels. To Goering we owe the discovery of simple pomp, to Hitler that of voluntary compulsion, and Goebbels has produced the true lie." On another occasion a popular comedian appears on the stage. The lights go out all over the house. "Who is the idiot", he exclaims, "who has plunged us all in darkness?" He produces a torch, stoops down into the auditorium and flashes it in the faces of several people in the stalls. "No", he cries, "it isn't you, or you … or you … *So muss er wieder an der Leitung Liegen.*" This is a play on words, the meaning being either "It must be the power-station", or "It's the Government again."

All the evidence points to the existence within Germany itself of an undercurrent of opposition. But it is found almost exclusively among middle-aged people who have had actual experience of war. These as a body are regarded as unreliable. It was known that in the event of war last autumn the older men would be sent to the front in order to meet the fate of Uriah the Hittite. There was no popular enthusiasm as the troop trains left for the Eastern frontier. But among young people there is no such reluctance to force the issue. Removed as they are, so far as is possible, from the politically disintegrating influences of home life and the Christian religion, they are imbued at school with a zeal to spread the new Gospel. They are convinced that they will meet with little resistance, and this conviction is deepened by the many concessions that have already been made and by the disparagement of their opponents which, in spite of Hitler's own warning in *Mein Kampf* is now the order of the day. For this, the pre-Munich policy of Great Britain and France is largely responsible. Now that the shiftiness and perfidy of the German Government is openly revealed, the opposition both within and without Germany has been greatly strengthened, morally as well as materially. If Germany wants more, she must get it quickly. For Germany it is a question of gaining ground without losing time: for her adversaries it is one of gaining time without losing ground.

The next few months will be crucial. Possibly some pretext for another military demonstration may be found or provoked as soon as the harvest is gathered in. If the German army were the author and not merely the instrument of German policy, the peace of the world would not be seriously threatened. Neither the march into Austria nor the final invasion of Czecho-Slovakia commended itself to the General Staff. But Hitler felt sure that the mere display of force would ensure a bloodless victory. He was right. Will he be right again? The temper of the world has changed: in spite of her huge territorial gains, the destruction of the Czech defences and the appropriation of Czech arms, aeroplanes and munition factories, Germany is unlikely to be given another chance of swallowing her unresisting neighbours piecemeal. She will have to fight, and to fight on more than one front. It is doubtful whether she has the necessary material resources. It is doubtful, too, whether she has the necessary brains. Educational standards have declined, and the officers and N.C.Os. of the conscript army are not up to the standard of the professional Reichswehr.

The Germans of today fall naturally into two groups. Some, if the Ministry of Propaganda chooses to say so, are credulous enough to believe that two and two make twenty-two: others have become so sceptical that if Dr. Goebbels declared that two and two make four, their first impulse would be to doubt it.

1999

Alf Tressler, as he was known in the School, taught modern languages. He was an Alsatian by birth, and was therefore fluent in French and German. He was a bachelor, who lived in a small house, half way up Charterhouse Hill. He was a small, precise, and outspoken man, a great disciplinarian, and could put the fear of God into you, if you crossed him.

His form room was decorated with Biblical sayings, such as "Who can tell how oft he offendeth", (quite often in my case), and he took me for extra German, which I hated, out of school hours.

He was a great admirer of his fellow Alsatian, Albert Schweitzer, a Nobel Prizewinner, who ran a leper colony in Africa, so we used to have to listen to a lot about him.

Despite his perhaps frightening exterior and firm discipline, he had a kind heart, and when I got to know him, I liked and respected him. It was his European bicycle tours in the holidays for which many will remember him. I went with him in 1938 to Venice, and in 1939 to Florence, in the Easter holidays. He would take us (8 or 9 boys) by train to some convenient place in Switzerland or France, and from there we would set off on our bicycles, our meagre luggage on a carrier over the front wheel, and cover about 80–100 miles a day, according to the terrain. After breakfast, he would say, "we are going to so and so for tonight, I will meet you there" and then he would set off, the boys straggling along behind. If there were interesting places on the way, he would stop and tell us about them, otherwise we went more or less as we wished in two's or three's, secure in the knowledge that our fathers had given us an allowance of £1 per day to cover accommodation and food. In those days it was just enough.

At one time, with one other boy, Colin Drury, we arrived at our rendezvous, but Alf and the others didn't turn up until nearly two days later, and naturally we were worried, with very little money, and not speaking Italian. When Alf did arrive, he only stopped for a minute or so, and then rode off again. (During the war, Colin became an ADC to General Montgomery in the Desert – perhaps these travel experiences with a difficult man, helped him in his relations with another difficult man.)

On arrival at our final destination, for a few days of sightseeing and talks from Alf, we went back to England by train. This marvellous, uncomfortable, almost unsupervised, bicycling holiday in a foreign country, before the days of mass travel, was very good for us, and taught us to be more independent, resourceful and less narrow minded than we might have been, with our limited experience of life.

Alfred William Tressler came to Charterhouse in 1906, and retired in 1940.

However, he came back to the School, to teach, in 1940-45.

He died in Godalming in 1951.

I shall always remember him as a good and kind man.

Thomas Day – 1748-1789

by Sir Samuel Scott

In the year 1757 a stolid little boy of nine years of age appeared at Charterhouse. This was the usual age for entrance to a public-school. The little boy was called Thomas Day, destined to make some mark as a political writer, but now remembered only as the author of a famous children's book – "Sandford and Merton."

The old monastic buildings of Charterhouse must have looked rather grim, and the life was to be a hard one. But we must not think of old Charterhouse as isolated among business premises and the picturesque but rather slummy old streets that are fast disappearing. The City was still a residential area where business people had their homes. Westminster, which comprises the greater part of the London that we know to-day, was still a kind of fashionable suburb; and the aristocratic squares of Bloomsbury had not yet been built. The School, just outside the City wall, was in the heart of things.

When little Thomas arrived he found a School with forty black-robed "gownboys" on the foundation. But Thomas was not one of these; he had been left a rich little boy on the death of his father and so was ineligible to be a "gownboy". There were about a hundred day-boys and boarders, and Day was one of these.

The boarders lived in the Matron's house or with the Master, and perhaps escaped some of the rigours endured by the gownboys.

But presumably they kept the same hours, rising at five, with school from six in the morning till six at night. At ten o'clock an usher went round the gownboys' dormitory to see that they were safely tucked up, two in a bed. The food was atrocious, and remained so until recent times. As late as the "sixties" of the last century the boys were half-starved. The commons of bread was a pittance and "the meat often putrid and always bad". The wretched gownboys were so hungry in the 18th century that a little before Day's time they had mutinied and were locked in the School building until they gave in from sheer starvation. The Master, who was assisted by an usher, an assistant usher and a writing master, was a certain Dr. Crusius, presumably of German origin. According to all accounts he applied Germanic discipline to his charges. That applied only to discipline in School. Outside School hours a collection of young savages did pretty much as they pleased. There were no organized games, and as there were no playing fields in the middle of London, we can assume that there was no cricket; football was a rough and tumble affair with no referee's whistle. The great game then was bowling hoops and having races, driving four hoops at a time, past the Chapel cloisters to the finishing post.

We must not, of course, suppose that Charterhouse was any worse than any other public school. The other three great Schools – Eton, Westminster and Winchester – were certainly no better. The horrors of Long Chamber at Eton are notorious, and Sydney Smith has told us what Winchester was like in the early 19th century. To have been a scholar at any time can only have been a purgatory; for a commoner things were probably better, especially if a boy had plenty of money to buy food and was fitted to stand up for himself. The famous Lord Melbourne looked back on his Eton days as the happiest of his life, and Day himself, one of our earliest educationalists, seems to have made no complaints about Charterhouse, and certainly was not a protagonist in the campaign for the reform of public schools. Young Thomas was a big hulking lad and was one of the best boxers in the School. Organized fights with bare fists were a regular proceeding, as they were until recent times in every school, and the gloves which the late Lord Queensberry described euphemistically as "feather-beds" were unknown.

Master Thomas was a very odd boy – odder then than he would be to-day. He was rich and generous; he kept a fund for charitable objects and was frequently taken in; he was interested in birds and flowers, which was not then called "Nature Study", and in the days when no boy had any idea of birds-nesting except to take the clutch of eggs or to throw out the nestlings, he had a tender feeling for wild life. He was of a generous nature in other ways too. Altogether he was an unnaturally virtuous boy, a complete prig, and even at that time must have been a bore. But in spite of all this, there was something about young Thomas that made him likeable.

At Oxford, Day developed into an eccentric. The Universities were at a low ebb; the Fellows of Colleges were sunk in bibulous sloth, while the undergraduates spent most of their time in rather disreputable amusements. Day, on the contrary, made the discovery that the pursuit of virtue is the only aim – an admirable conclusion. But he overlooked the "sixth rule" of a celebrated man (the other five rules being non-existent) "Don't take yourself too seriously." To the end of his life Day took himself very seriously indeed.

On leaving Oxford he read for the Bar, believing, as enlightened people did at the time, that mankind could be made virtuous by the right legislation. At the same time he made the acquaintance of his life-long friend, Richard Lovell Edgeworth, father of the famous Maria – a gay spark who provides an extraordinary foil to the virtuous Day.

Day perceived that he must embark on matrimony if he was to lead a full and useful life. But his wife must be adapted to his peculiar ideas, combining the virtues of the Spartan maid and the Roman matron, despising frivolities and leading a life of simplicity and devotion to good works. The philosopher searched in vain for a lady worthy to be united with him, and therefore embarked on the maddest of his schemes – to train up two little Foundling girls in his own ideas, one of whom surely would turn out to be all that he hoped. Naturally, the plan was a complete failure. One little girl was incurably naughty from the start, the other failed to pass Day's exacting tests when she was in her teens – the fortitude which Day demanded was clearly lacking. This was shown when Day fired pistols, charged with blank, at her petticoats and dropped hot sealing wax on her neck and arms. The wretched girl simply screamed – and was dismissed. In any case Day had decided that he wanted to marry another young lady, the beautiful Honora Sneyd. And when Honora refused to comply with his pedantic and impossible conditions he transferred his affections to her still more beautiful sister Elizabeth. Day was now so desperately in love that he threw overboard all his previous principles, gave up his eccentric dress and went to France (as the custom then was) to be made into a polished gentleman. He endured much in the process – even sitting for days in a wooden vice in a vain endeavour to straighten his knock knees. He came back to claim Elizabeth, dressed in the fantastic fashion of the time, with a towering wig and bowing and scraping like a dancing master. Elizabeth couldn't help laughing, and there was an end of it for the unfortunate suitor.

Day had given up his most cherished principles for the sake of a pretty girl. But he recovered and returned to his political interests. He opposed the political corruption of the time, he hated slavery and wrote a poem that had some celebrity about the sorrows of a negro slave. Not long after this time the American War of Independence began. Day, like many of the better people in this country, was violently on the side of the Colonials. Again he rushed into verse, indignant at the outrages said to have been committed by our troops.

Meanwhile, a lady had been discovered by Day's friend, the

excellent Dr. Small, who seemed to fulfil all the requirements. In due course Day married her, having first of all ascertained that she was high-minded in every way and was ready to fall in with all his eccentric ideas. Strange as it may seem, it is fair to say that his wife was devoted to him and inconsolable when he died. Under the softening influence of marriage, Day mellowed to some extent and became less extreme. The couple led a solitary life in the remote country, where Day tried his hand at farming. But he and his wife gave themselves up to doing good among the poor people around them, and there is no doubt that they were greatly loved.

By this time Day had given up his political work. He was associated with the more extreme partisans of reform and democracy. Certainly, there was much that needed reform; Parliament was hopelessly corrupt and elections were carried by bribery on an enormous scale. Day spoke at meetings, showing considerable courage. The French Revolution had created a dread of extremists, and Day and his friends ran the risk of imprisonment by their outspoken denunciations. As a pamphleteer he had considerable notoriety, and Pitt himself, who was toying with the idea of reform, invited Day to stand for Parliament. He declined to do so, perhaps wisely, for he was too scrupulous to stoop to the methods of politicians. We may laugh at Day as a portentous prig and an unconscionable bore, but we have to admit that he was far ahead of his time in many ways, and invariably kind-hearted and generous. He met his death in a tragic way. One of his beliefs was that anything could be done with animals by kindness. But his confidence in an unbroken colt was misplaced. He was thrown and killed on the spot at the early age of 41, sincerely mourned by many.

The book by which Day is known to posterity – "Sandford and Merton" – did not come out till the last year or two of his life. Generations of children, down to quite recent times, have been brought up on it and enjoyed it. It is didactic and sententious, after the manner of all children's books of the time, but it is just the sort of thing to please a child. With all his priggishness and quaint ideas, Day liked children, and was liked by them.

1999

Sir Samuel Haslam Scott, Bart, who wrote a biography of Thomas Day in 1935, called "The Exemplary Mr Day", died in 1960, and was succeeded by his son Oliver, who was in Gownboys in 1939 when I left.

Bogey

by Henry Longhurst

In the history of school golfing societies, none has had anything approaching the success enjoyed by the Old Carthusians. Why? Heaven only knows. I often wonder myself.

The team which habitually wins the Halford Hewitt Cup at Deal, against sides that, on paper, look a good deal stronger is a mixed collection whose principal virtue is that they all get on well with each other. They are probably the only team in the tournament who would not mind having their various foursome partnerships drawn out of a hat.

Let me tell you something about a few of them, since perhaps you only know them from reading their names in the newspapers.

First, and essentially part of the team, is Mr. Hewitt, the Donor, who was in Duckites. He has now reached the ripe age of 70 but doesn't look it. Significantly the only occasion on which we have not won the tournament in the past six years was when he was unable to be there. How his temper or his physique stands this week each year at Deal defeats me, for his leg is pulled mercilessly from the moment he arrives. Perhaps it is explained by a remark he made to me when I was thanking him for a week-end at his lovely home in Suffolk: "Never mind, my boy," he said, "I'd do anything for Charterhouse!"

The trainer of the team is Ben Travers, writer of the Aldwych farces and almost the best after-dinner speaker I ever heard. His duty is to see the team get up in the morning, provide them with fruit salts, and carry round flasks of Cherry Brandy and Kummel with which to encourage them at the 7th and 12th holes.

The team themselves embrace a variety of callings. Dale Bourn, captain for the past two years, now works with the Greyhound Racing Association. John Beck, captain of Britain's Walker Cup team, is a business man who travels all over Europe and is well known, with Ben Travers, as an after-dinner speaker.

Lionel Burdon Sanderson, so far as one can gather, spends most of his time hunting big game or living in a caravan. Pat White is a product of Mr Oswald Latter and now science master at Harrow. The enormous Cecil Middleton is an accountant working at the moment in Glasgow, while Jack Thompson farms the richest land in England, up by the Wash. He flies his own airplane and is one of the best shots in the country. John Morrison spends half his time designing golf courses and the rest competing with me in golf journalism.

For the past six years John and I have played amicably in the bottom – pardon, I mean "root" foursome and only once have we been beaten. He uses a fearful set of ancient rusty clubs, some with handles as thick as a cricket bat, and his style is not exactly the one laid down in the text books; but he's a fine cheerful partner and he holes the doubtful putts. If you play golf, you will know how much that means.

Before he starts in the morning he has what he calls "fifty up" on the practice ground with a gadget known as a "swing controller". It involves strapping on a belt round one's middle and fixing a string attached to the belt to the end of one's club. Whether it really controls his swing is another matter.

I am, as I say increasingly baffled year by year to know why this odd collection should regularly win one of the most eagerly coveted honours in amateur golf. But they do, and what's more I think they will go on doing so. Let us leave it at that.

1999

Henry C. Longhurst was born in 1909 and left Gownboys in 1927 to go up to Cambridge. He was Captain of the University Golf Club in 1931, and Amateur Champion in 1936. He became a journalist, author and broadcaster. During WWII he joined the Army, in the Royal Artillery.

In 1943–45 he was the M.P. for the Acton Division of Middlesex.

He won the "Journalist of the Year" award in 1969, and was made C.B.E. in 1972.

Tunisian Scenes

by Henry Baerlein

There has been a good deal of talk – and it will end in nothing else – by Italians with reference to Tunis. There is a large number of Italians there; in Soho the number of Italians is not insignificant, and there is an equal probability that France and Great Britain will decline to hand over either of those two places. One should not forget that the African inhabitants of Tunis are overwhelmingly in favour of the French Protectorate. They are well aware of Italy's colonial methods, which were exposed to a horrified world in the book of a young Danish traveller, Holmbue by name, who, with an American companion and an Arab boy, journeyed all through North Africa a few years ago. The Italians, with a notable exception now and then, viewed him with deep suspicion, chiefly because he could speak Arabic. If they had known what kind of a book he was going to write they would have expelled him much sooner, for he showed how some 12,000 natives, a year, were being executed by that same Marshal Graziani, who afterwards continued these pacifying methods in Abyssinia, that country which hangs like a mill-stone round Italy's neck. All the Italian demands for Tunis will be rejected. So let us turn away from politics and have a look at some aspects of that interesting land. Morocco, Algiers, Tunis – that is the French Empire of Northern Africa from West to East.

In Tunis, the capital, as well as in other towns of the Protectorate, the French have been wise enough to build the European quarter away from the Native town, so that the picturesque appearance of the latter is not impaired.

The covered-in bazaars, the so-called "souks", of Tunis are a labyrinth in which you wander, fascinated – through the "souk" El-Attarine, where perfume vendors in their tiny shops sit meditating; where the merchants of long wedding-candles gaze at you, and where the dealers in brightly-coloured Kairouan carpets will be glad if you step in to pass the time of day with them. There is the "souk" of Belghas, where the tribe of shoe-makers is cutting-out and hammering and sewing all the day to turn out their gay-coloured slippers. And the saddler's "souk", which has been famous from the thirteenth century, with the tomb of a holy man, a marabout, who was a saddler. Perhaps one steps into an Arab cafe, say the cafe des Marabouts, in order to escape for a moment from the thronging, good-natured crowd.

Carpeted benches invite you to rest and take your coffee, but although only a few customers may be squatting on the central platform (and two of them playing a game of cards so simple that it may supersede baccarat or chemin-de-fer) it is impossible that you will stay for more than a couple of minutes, for a swarthy individual, from whose ear a delicate white flower is hanging, sits upon his haunches just beside the players and produces from a comb a kind of music which encourages, it seems, the two card-players, but will scarcely send a shiver of delight through anyone who hears it for the first time.

Where will it be possible to find, here in the Arab parts of Tunis, an oasis, as it were, of silence? We pass by Bab-Souika, the market-place, with its masses of vermilion fruits, of green vegetables, of onions tinted like violets, and long loaves, which in the oven, have been baked a pallid gold. We come by chance to the Court of the Cadi, a beautiful building, three centuries old. The actual courtyard is filled with lawyers, who discuss their business under the white and black arches, or as they lean against the walls of blue-brown tiles. At the right of the entrance is a row of veiled women in their voluminous white robes; they are waiting to be divorced, and they know that the most they can hope for from the brief ceremony is – if they can demonstrate their perfect innocence – to have their dowry returned to them . . . At the far end of the little courtyard is a room, around three sides of which there runs a bench of brilliant green upholstery, while in the centre of the middle wall, the bench is interrupted by a large green, gilded throne which is, very occasionally, occupied by his Highness the Bey. But this morning the administration of Arab justice – there is also a French Court and a mixed tribunal – is going to be undertaken by even other judges. As each one arrives and solemnly, rather wearily, advances through the courtyard, he is greeted by the litigants with the utmost respect and, more or less gracefully, he submits to his hand or his sleeve being kissed. He thereupon steps into the judgment room, kicks off his yellow slippers, is supplied by the attendant with a softer pair and then, as he sinks down on to the green bench, he tucks his legs under him. Then the barristers and their clients come in and settle down immediately opposite the judges. Apparently the proceedings at one end of the room do not incommode the occupants of the other end. It is lawful for you to watch them through a glass window, and you see that in this court of civil justice – the criminal court in another street is a veritable pandemonium – you see that they can get on very well indeed without silence. The cadis are either amused at a witticism or are talking, two of them at the same time, to the barristers, or are offering each other snuff. The barristers lean forward and talk confidentially with the judges, while the litigants are at liberty, it seems, to take a part, whenever they desire to do so, in the general conversation

* * *

There is a tale in Tunis with regard to what occurred when, in the latter half of the nineteenth century, his Highness the Bey had been saluted by a British man-of-war. He sent his leading admiral to Malta to return the compliment. This journey is accomplished now by ordinary steamers in about twelve hours. That admiral, however, was away from Tunis for a month and, on returning, told his Highness that there was no Malta; he had cruised about in all directions and had given up all hope of finding it . . . Between the sixteenth and eighteenth centuries the men of Tunis had a far more intimate acquaintance with the Mediterranean, for they revelled in piracy. England had to bear, like other countries, many insults and extortions at the hands of the Tunisian pirates. But, in spite of this, she coveted their friendship, as she had no harbour in that sea, where it was possible for ships to be re-victualled or repaired.

His Highness the Bey is always an elderly gentleman, for the succession is not from father to son, but to the eldest surviving male of the royal family. As a rule the Bey lives in his palace at La Marsa, a few miles from his capital, where delicate white houses are almost hidden in the palm trees and where one has glimpses of the dazzling sea and of the beautiful red cliffs. But on the eve of Ramedan, one morning, the amiable old Bey (who had lately taken to himself another wife, a lady of about eighteen) came to the town where in his ancestral palace he proposed to affix his seal to a large number of documents and also to arrange about his visits to the various mosques in Ramedan. A motley, good-natured crowd of nondescript Arabs, among them a few black-veiled women, French gendarmerie in their sombre uniforms and some exalted Tunisians, awaited the ruler. These exalted ones greeted each other in the customary fashion with kisses and, while they stood about the doorway of the palace they were not above exchanging a few words with a couple of famous beggars, one of them with a distorted mouth and a very roguish expression, the other with a mop of tangled hair, a garment of sacking and – it is said – a large balance at his bankers . . .

Several French gendarmes arrived on bicycles, and after them some Tunisian horsemen. Meanwhile, perhaps, a score of cavalrymen in blue and red, belonging to the Bey's private army, had taken up a position in the square; they presented arms as a herald on a white horse came upon the scene. This elderly gentleman seemed to be very dissatisfied, as he was absolutely roaring certain words. But these, being translated, were: "Salutation and Benediction!" He was uttering them on behalf of the Bey and the black-veiled women twittered their hands, while the men bowed gravely. As the herald is a personage who was originally introduced by the Turks, it is the custom for him to pronounce those words in Arabic indeed, but with a Turkish accent. Behind him in the first carriage there comes another importation from Turkey, His Highness's principal dwarf, a middle-aged gentleman who was once a schoolmaster at Istanbul and is now reputed to keep the Bey in continual laughter. The Bey possesses six other dwarfs, two women and four men, of whom it is not demanded that they shall be witty or even funny. They are kept because the Beys have always had such persons in their household. Several other carriages roll up, with State officials and some of the rather woe-begone princes, who have little to do except to live and to be present at ceremonies. Finally, drawn by six fine mules, there comes the carriage of the Bey. The postilions, men well over six feet, and the drivers are clad in gorgeous liveries of sky blue and gold brocade. The Bey has with him all his Ministers – the Prime Minister, the Minister of the Pen, and the Minister of Justice. (All the other portfolios are held by the French.) Then the Bey, amid the acclamations of the bystanders, emerges from his carriage and, on the arm of his burly, bearded Prime Minister, he enters the palace.

* * *

When you set sail from the mainland of Tunis you will arrive in about an hour, if you are lucky, on the exquisite isle of Djerba. The camels that go to and fro are normally put upon a separate ship and are tied down with quantities of string, as they are nervous seafarers and try to throw themselves overboard. They look despairingly across the waste of waters and produce a noise midway between that of an outraged lion and an agitated sheep. The other passengers are mostly Arabs wrapped up in their Biblical apparel; they lie down and many of them draw their robes across their faces until happily the vessel reaches El Kantara, the little southern port. If you remember that this island was the place where medieval pirates used to congregate, you will be asking why they did not seek an island with a cliff or mountain where they could defend themselves. Apparently they did not have to do so. In the service of the Bey and for their own personal advantage, they would ply their trade and unmolested, come to Djerba to recuperate. When the Spaniards built their two great fortresses that still remain, the pirates did not lead such easy lives; but even then they could not keep away from Djerba . . . Homer tells us that this is the home of the Lotophagi; and the botanists of our own day have done their best to ascertain which of the multitude of Djerba's flowers is the ancient lotus. But the companions of Ulysses were enchanted, it is probable, by the delights which everywhere surrounded them and, in the symbolic language of the time, were said to have partaken of the lotus. Nowadays, the Djerbans are as mild as mild; in fact the Moslems, who are in the great majority, are much devoted to the grocer's trade. Nearly all the grocers in the Protectorate of Tunis hail from Djerba; in Istanbul and Morocco and the intervening countries, many Djerban grocers may be found. They have the one ambition to make so much money that they can retire and buy a property upon the island. Hence the price of land has risen vastly, but the grocers do not care a bit. They build among the palms their snow-white houses, some of which are very splendid.

* * *

Let us go back to the capital and to a coffee-house, which has existed in its present shape for three centuries and has the peculiar attraction of the tombs of certain marabouts, a father and two sons, which stand in a large alcove. They are wooden tombs, all painted red and green, while red and green flags are suspended over them and names appear upon the tombs, but those of the three marabouts are not forgotten, though they flourished in the fourteenth century. At that time there existed on this site another coffee-house, whose customers were entertained and edified by the performances of these good men. They came as near to Allah as they could, by dancing vehemently in his honour and declining to commit themselves to any other trade. So much is known of them; but also it may be that they pleased the audience by letting swords (apparently) transfix their bodies, by seeming to devour cactus leaves, by munching mica made to look like glass, and so forth. Anyhow, it happens ever autumn that their brotherhood sends to the coffee-house expert musicians who, on Thursday evenings, for several weeks, play on their drums and flutes and bagpipes, and sing their falsetto songs to celebrate the season of the anniversary of marabout pere . . . During the remainder of the year the clients of this coffee-house are satisfied to listen to a gramophone. Such are the Arab powers of concentration that one sometimes sees a coffee-house on a far smaller scale in which are three or four gramophones all playing Arab music simultaneously. In front of each of them there is an ardent group of the admirers of that special song, who sit there on their haunches and are perfectly delighted. They have achieved the very enviable habit of not hearing what they do not want to hear. But in the venerable coffee-house we have been talking of, the music is subsidiary to the games of cards. On a platform, two or three feet from the ground, the players are engaged in what does not appear a very complicated game. Occasionally they accuse each other in the shrillest tones, of having cheated, or of having tried to do so, and the audience, squatting round them like so many monkeys, much enjoy these little episodes.

* * *

On the electric tram-line from Tunis to La Marsa, and some eight miles from the capital, is the British Consulate, a large house, many years ago allotted to us by a friendly Bey. It has a private station where the trams will only stop if they are asked to do so. After nightfall, this is done by lighting from the house a row of lamps along the avenue and one, a red one, over the small platform. In this pleasant country house the Consul-General lives the whole year round; his office is in Tunis. And in the house I found an excellent example of the variegated nature of the population of this French Protectorate. Many, many years ago, a Consul's wife came with a maid whose home was Finland; she acquired in Tunis an Arabian husband, who had been the cook of an Italian gentleman, had been with him in Italy and learned the language. This Finn-Arabian couple, who addressed each other in Italian, had been in the service of successive British Consuls and their wives. Unfortunately, they had not been blessed with children, but they were a good example of the way in which the country is composed of divers races . . . Nearly all the members of the British colony are Maltese, who flock to the Consul's magnificent garden to celebrate the King's Birthday. Scarcely any of them can talk English, but they are extremely proud of the fact that they are British subjects.

1999

Henry P.B. Baerlein was born in 1875, and left Weekites in 1892 to go up to Cambridge.

He was the author of over forty books, and contributed many articles to the national newspapers and magazines.

In the Great War, he served with the British Ambulance Committee in France.

He died in 1960.

CHAPTER II

"The Three Editors", Sixty Years On

MOSS, GIBSON, BRAY

Major I.W.S. MOSS M.C. & Bar, Coldstream Guards

Bill Moss was a good looking young man (Sir Iain Moncreiffe described him later, as "tall and devilish languid".) His father was English and travelled abroad a lot on his business, and his mother was Russian. He was born in Japan, and two years later, he and his family survived a devastating earthquake there.

His background was therefore very cosmopolitan, quite different from my own very english background.

He was artistic and romantic in his outlook and interests, a modern edition of Dumas' Musketeer.

Like myself, he was not a scholar or great games player, and our "studies" in Gownboys were next to each other, so that we became firm friends.

After leaving Charterhouse at the end of the Summer Quarter 1939, Bill went off to Latvia (perhaps to see relations on his mother's side) and on the outbreak of war in September, he sailed a boat back to England, and enlisted in the Coldstream Guards as a volunteer.

After training at Caterham, he was commissioned as an Ensign, and was eventually posted to the 3rd Battalion of the Coldstream Guards in North Africa, just before Montgomery's successful campaign against Rommel.

He appears then to have been recruited into the Special Operations Executive, based in Cairo.

Their headquarters was in a villa called "Tara", on the outskirts, and there was assembled a strange group of individuals, who later made their names in clandestine operations behind the enemy lines.

These people included Billy Maclean, David Smiley, Xan Fielding, Patrick Leigh Fermor, and Countess Sophie Tarnowska from Poland, whom Bill Moss eventually married.

It must have been a very strange and interesting household.

Bill Moss

It was there that Bill Moss and Paddy Leigh Fermor discussed and evolved a plan, to parachute into Crete, which was still held by the Germans, kidnap the German General commanding the troops there, and bring him back alive to Cairo.

The Germans may have occupied and controlled Crete, but it is a mountainous island, the Cretans were not docile, but very independently minded and aggressive, and so the Germans were very much a beleaguered occupying force. Paddy and Bill's plan was to work very closely with the Cretan Partisan forces.

Paddy was to parachute into the island first, on February 4th, and organise the resistance, and Bill was to follow by parachute a little later. Whilst Paddy landed successfully, Bill tried about 12 times, but the weather always closed in and they had to return to Cairo, but eventually he went in by naval boat, and arrived there on April 4th, 1943, to find Paddy waiting for him with a motley collection of Cretan Irregulars.

The German they were after was General Kreipe, commanding 10,000 German troops based at Heraklion, but living in the Villa Ariadne on the outskirts, and travelling to and fro by car, daily, to his Headquarters.

The General was very regular in his habits, and the plan was to hijack him one evening, outside Heraklion on his way home, spirit him away to the mountains and hide him in caves there, until they could get him down to a safe beach, and rendezvous with a naval vessel, to get him back to the North African shore, and so to Cairo. Easy to state as a plan, but much more difficult to actually carry it out, and even more so, to carry it out successfully. That it was successful, had an element of luck, but was also due to excellent planning, and considerable bravery by the persons concerned. It was therefore on April 26th 1943, that everyone was in place and waiting for the General to be driven from his H.Q. to his home. At strategic places along the route, the Partisans were hidden and could signal the progress of the General's car, to a crossroads, where Paddy and Bill waited, dressed in German

W.S.M. ('. . . an Englishman dressed up as a German leaning against the bar at the Berkeley') and Paddy ('. . . so much the dashing Teuton that beside him one felt uncomfortably close to the genuine article')

uniforms, and supported in the background by a force of Cretan Partisans, armed to the teeth, ready to put the well drilled plan into action. The General was a bit late in leaving his H.Q., and it was already dark, but gradually his progress was reported, and at 9.30 p.m. the warning buzzer went off, and Paddy and Bill stationed themselves in the road and switched on the red light to halt the car at the junction. The car stopped, and they walked slowly towards it, Bill on the driver's side, and Paddy on the other, their pistols cocked in their hands behind their backs.

Suddenly, everything happened. The Partisans came out of hiding, the car doors were wrenched open, Bill coshed the chauffeur before he could reach his gun, and he was heaved out of the car. At the same time Paddy and his helpers pulled the General out of the car and subdued him.

Bill then got into the driver's seat, the General was bundled into the back and sat on by three of the Partisans, who held a knife to his throat, to stop him shouting, and Paddy, wearing the General's hat, got into the front seat beside Bill, and off they went towards Heraklion, through which they had to drive, to get on to their escape road to the mountains. The first German road block came fairly soon, with a German sentry standing in the middle of the road, swinging a red lamp. Instead of stopping, they proceeded very slowly, so that the sentry could see the General's pennants on the wings of the car, and once past, they accelerated, and anxiously waited for the sentry to open fire, but he didn't. They went through the same routine with the next twenty control posts, until they were entering Heraklion, where they encountered large numbers of German troops and lorries going to a cinema performance in the town. Having negotiated the Main Square, they had to pass through the West Gate, a massive narrow stone structure, with a German guard on duty, who signalled them to stop. They slowed to a snail's pace, and as the sentry moved forward to interrogate them Paddy lowered the window and called out in German that this was the General's car, and Bill accelerated. The sentries seemed taken aback, but everyone saluted, and Paddy called "Gute Nacht", and they got away into the open country.

After a further nearly two hours' drive, they stopped, and Bill got out with the General and two of the Partisans, and set off across country to a cave in the mountains, while Paddy went on to dump the car, and to find his way back to Bill and the General, in their previously planned hiding place.

Throughout the period of hiding in caves, and the long march to the get away beach, the General became quite philosophical, and gradually came to terms with his predicament, but insisted that he was not left alone with the Partisans!

In order to try and protect the Cretans from the wrath of the Germans at the kidnap of the General, Paddy and Bill had left behind in the car some of their British uniform, and a carefully worded note to the Germans, saying that it was a British raiding party who were responsible, and not the local people. Unfortunately that didn't stop the Germans from massacring a lot of Cretans in their blind fury.

They also turned the island upside down in their search for the General and his captors, but the Partisans passed their friends and the General from cave to cave, and it was not until May 14th that they were finally able to rendezvous with the British Navy, on a beach on the south of the island, and get away with their now pacified quarry to Mersa Matruh and Cairo, and for Paddy and Bill to get back to Tara, where the rejoicing was great.

For their exploit Paddy was awarded a D.S.O., and Bill an M.C.

Their exploit was described as one of the finest true adventure stories of the last war, and Bill wrote his account of it, from his diaries, in "Ill Met by Moonlight", which was also made into a film. It is a book well worth reading.

Bill went back to Crete again later in 1944, and carried out a successful ambush of a German column, knocking out several of

Vassily *W.S.M.* *Ivan*

their trucks, and an armoured car, killing many soldiers, and taking several prisoners.

For this he was awarded a bar to his M.C.

However, things were changing in Crete, and the Communists were gaining power, and Bill suddenly found that some of the Communists were plotting to capture him, and "sell" him to the Germans. He therefore had to leave quickly.

After this second visit to Crete, Bill was sent to Macedonia, where he was attached to a division of Communist Guerrillas, who engaged in a war of sabotage of the German occupying forces. When the Germans finally retreated from Greece, the Greek Civil War broke out, and Bill went back to Cairo.

The inhabitants of Tara dispersed for leave and other ventures, Bill married Sophie, and the war in Europe came to an end.

Not so Bill's war – there were still the Japanese and, in May 1945, Bill was parachuted into Siam, with two other companions. They proceeded up country, expecting trouble, but the Japanese war was petering out, and there was no further fighting. Bill's mission was finished by the end of the year, and he prepared to go back to Cairo for Christmas, but was held up by civil disturbances.

He wrote a second book about his war, called "A War of Shadows", and as with the first one, it is very well written and interesting.

It is difficult to map Bill's life after that. He wrote two novels, "Bats with Baby Faces", and "The Hour of Flight", which were published, and then seems to have travelled a lot in Europe with Sophie. They produced two children and were reported as living in Ireland, sailing in the Mediterranean, and, finally, living in Jamaica, where Bill did some more writing, and died there, in 1965, at the age of 44.

The following Obituary appeared in the "Daily Gleaner" of Kingston, Jamaica – I think it reads as if it was written by Bill himself!

Stratis Manoli 'Wallace Beery' George 'Nikko'
Grigori P.M.L.-F. W.S.M.

The abduction gang

W.S.M. General Kreipe P.M.L.-F.

MOSS – On August 9th, 1965, at his home at Hermitage, Kingston, Jamaica, Ivan William Stanley Moss, aged 44

The following is printed from a local paper:-

'He was born a little over forty-four years ago in Yokohama, Japan, during the great earthquake, the only child of an English multi-millionaire (steel magnate), diplomat father who lost his fortune on Wall Street in 1929, and a White Russian refugee mother. By the age of six, he had travelled two-and-a-half times around the world.

'He was holidaying in Latvia immediately after his graduation from Charterhouse and about to enter Oxford when World War II broke out. He then found himself obliged to cross the North Sea in a yacht. After this voyage, it was joining the Queen's own "Coldstream Guard". As a Guards Officer, he dined at Chequers and the Court of St. James. He has smoked opium in a Siamese den and sweated it out in the French Foreign Legion dives of Siddi-bel-Abbes.

'He has eaten pemmican in the Antarctic and caviar in the palaces of the mid-Orient. He has gorged himself on plankton in mid-ocean, lived off grubs in the jungle, and sampled the fare in the most exclusive eating places the world over, and he has savoured red herring, soaked in white rum and set alight, in the Jamaican mountains. Also, as a member of Winston Spencer Churchill's entourage, he lived at Chequers.

'During World War II, one of his many exploits with the Secret Service was, as a Captain, he had the heroic and heralded feat of not only capturing the German General who commanded the German forces on the island of Crete, but also crossing the island and rendezvousing with an allied submarine to effect the General's abduction to Great Britain. After this perilous feat, he saw secret service in Macedonia, Algeria, Siam, France, Germany, Holland, Belgium, Italy, etc. His factual account of the General's capture became a world best seller when he wrote "Ill Met by Moonlight". Another best seller was "Bats with Baby Faces".

'As Major Moss, he was in pursuit of war criminals throughout the world. One, Otto Scrozeny, who captured Benito Mussolini on an Alp mountain during World War II – which was one of the War's greatest endeavours – was pursued and found by Major Moss in Spain for an exclusive interview.

'When these horizons began to pall, he inaugurated a polar air rescue service which led him, in 1957-58, to go parachuting in the Antarctic during the Fuchs-Hillary expeditions. There followed a year "Down Under". Next was New Zealand where he boarded a yacht and sailed to Nassau, Bahamas, via Tahiti. In Nassau, he wrote for the *Nassau Guardian* until he felt fleet of foot to bring down 1961 as his first year in Jamaica. His association was with the *Daily Gleaner*, the most widely read newspaper in the Caribbean, where he wrote the ever-popular column "Merry-Go-Round". His words were eagerly looked for from the one instalment to the next. Why? More than often the analyses were right.

'Just the other day, an editor said, "If I had the brains of Mr. Moss, I would not be working for this newspaper."'

Sir Ralph Gibson QC PC

The Right Honourable Sir RALPH GIBSON, Q.C, P.C.

Ralph has had a distinguished career since leaving Gownboys, but it is difficult to get him to write or talk about it. He is a very modest man, unlike Bill and I. The most that I could get from him was the following.

"I did not go straight into the forces in 1939 as you did. I had two terms at Brasenose College (but living in Christchurch) and then joined up and got sent to a Royal Armoured Corps OCTU whence I was posted to the King's Dragoon Guards in the Western Desert. Armoured cars commanded by rich, aristocratic, and immensely brave young men – for the most part. They were very nice to me. When the fighting ended in North Africa I was fortunate enough to be sent to the Trans Jordan Frontier Force, where I tried to learn Arabic, and to avoid provoking either side in Palestine, which was much nicer than going round corners in Italy. I got home early in May 1945 and an early release to go back to Oxford. Degree in law 1947. Bigelow Teaching Fellow at University of Chicago 1948–49. Ann came home with me in 1950, never having seen this country, and we have lived happily, if not very excitingly, ever since. We have a large 1895 flat hard by Westminster Cathedral. Our three children, with 6 grandchildren, all live in London. One barrister; one solicitor; one publisher's editor."

And his entry in "Who's Who" is equally short and dry, and hides a brilliant career at the Bar.

"GIBSON, Rt Hon Sir Ralph (Brian) P.C. 1985; Kt 1977; a Lord Justice of Appeal 1985-94; *b.* 17 Oct 1922; 2nd son of Roy and Emily Gibson; *m.* Ann Chapman Ruether, Chicago, one *s*, two *d*. *Educ.* Charterhouse, Brasenose Coll., Oxford (Hon Fellow 1986)".

THE BAR AS A PROFESSION

I was asked to write a note about the Bar because it was thought that it might be of interest to young people at Charterhouse who are close to the point of moving on to university and professional training. I was called to the Bar by the Middle Temple in June 1948. I had a second class degree in law from Oxford. I had no family connection with the law. I was admitted to common law chambers in London in 1950. I did mainly personal injury, insurance and trade union work; I was appointed Queen's Counsel in 1968; and became a Queen's Bench judge in 1977 and a Lord Justice in 1985. I retired in 1994. My experience is thus dated. Some of the rules relating to practice at the Bar have changed. The essential nature of the work has not.

There are two distinct aspects of the Bar as a profession to which I want to refer. The first is the idea, which is held by many, of an ancient profession, with fancy trappings and ranks and language, in which, for a few men of brilliance, glittering prizes may be won. In particular, it was said that men in wigs and gowns, with the rank of Queen's Counsel, earned huge fees.

This was always a sadly partial view of the Bar and its work. Furthermore, there were parts of that picture of the Bar which have long cried out for, and in some respects have received, reforming changes. There was recently a proposal for getting rid of the wearing of wigs. For my part I welcomed it. We can expect to see the proposal renewed. Next, it has been proposed that the institution of the rank of Queen's Counsel should be abolished; and that, if it is not to disappear entirely, it should cease to be in the gift of the Lord Chancellor, who is a member of the cabinet of the Government of the day, and should be conferred by an independent body within the profession itself under statutory guidelines. Further, and more importantly, for many years now such prizes as may be won by a barrister as a reward for skill and good fortune in the profession are as much open to be won by women as by men.

Of greatest importance, among proposed and pending changes, is the proposal for opening the right of audience in the higher courts to solicitors who satisfy certain requirements as to competence in advocacy. Full implementation of such proposals will probably reduce the amount of work available to the independent barrister, and in particular to the independent barrister recently started in the profession, as contrasted with the advocates employed by or belonging to a firm of solicitors. This is a matter of policy on which opinions may reasonably differ. It seems inevitable to me, and the better view, that such proposals will be implemented. If there are clear public benefits to be had from the existence of an independent Bar, made up of individual practitioners, as I believe there are, then, in my view, such an independent Bar can fairly be left to compete for work with advocates working for firms of solicitors.

The second aspect of the Bar as a profession, to which I now turn, is the nature of the main skill required for doing the job of a barrister. Some may have heard that to achieve real success at the Bar, among wigs and gowns in contests in court, a young woman or man must have a "gift for it" and must be adept at the "art of advocacy". Such people, thinking that they are probably not so endowed, may give up the idea of trying the Bar. And some very good people would be lost to the Bar who, if they started, would achieve success.

The main skill, to which I refer, is the ability to advise the client properly and to act for that client in accordance with his lawful instructions and the requirements of the law. If the barrister has the intellectual ability to learn and understand the relevant facts, as he is instructed, and to learn and understand the law relevant to those facts, he can advise the client. No gift of any art is required for this function. The ability can be commanded by native wit and hard work.

In much of the work done by barristers the giving of advice is the end of the matter. There will be no encounter in court in which any "art of advocacy" could be deployed. In most civil work, and in much of the criminal work, there is no jury and acting for the client means presenting his case to a judge or judges who will decide the issues. If the case is presented accurately and clearly it should fare as well in the process of decision as the merits of the case could require or justify. In most cases it will.

If there is a jury to decide issues of fact, in my experience the presentation of a case accurately and clearly will have the same effect. With or without a jury there may be "surprising" decisions which are explicable sometimes by simple error; and sometimes by asking who it is that feels surprise; and sometimes, it is said, by the triumph of the art of advocacy. The scope for this art is, in my view, at best minimal. Those who feel that they may not have it should pay to it no heed. They can function well on ability and hard work.

Anyone thinking of the Bar should have in mind that many barristers, after having practised for a time, move on to other work, for example in commerce or government, which for any reason seems attractive. This is not necessarily a matter of having failed at the Bar. Some simply want a change and are wise to seek it. The experience of work at the Bar will be of value in many other sorts of work.

My end is simple but important. I found life at the Bar to be good. I liked much of the work; I liked almost all the people with and against whom I did the work; I liked the judges before whom I appeared; and I greatly liked most of the places in which I did the work. The chambers to which I was first admitted were in the Temple in Garden Court; and after the war damage to Crown Office Row was repaired, I had a room there. Of course, many who like the work of the Bar do not want to do it in London. There are many agreeable places in which the chambers of barristers can be found. But the lawyer who spends most of his working life in and around the Inns of Court and the Royal Courts of Justice is fortunate indeed. Anyone thinking about the Bar should go and look.

Ralph Gibson
19 April 1999

MICHAEL BRAY D.S.C.

I came from a Charterhouse family, in that my father went to Girdlestoneites (Duckites) in about 1893, and I was preceded at Gownboys, by my two elder brothers. Several of my Girardot cousins were also at Charterhouse, and my daughter-in-law went to Gownboys. She now has three children, and it is my hope that at least one of them will go to Charterhouse in due course.

Unlike Robert Graves, I enjoyed my time at Charterhouse.

I suppose that I was a "middling" pupil, I certainly wasn't a scholar like Ralph Gibson, and left school from the Under Sixth, to go to Cambridge in the autumn of 1939, to read a "Mechanical Science Tripos". (I am never quite sure, now, why I chose this and I think that it was because I liked making things, and the other subjects didn't appeal.) Equally, I wasn't mad about team games, and played them because I had to. However, I could shoot straight with a rifle, and for my last year or two at Charterhouse, I was Captain of the Shooting VIII. In those days, there was a small bore range halfway down Racquets Court Hill, and for .303 rifles there was a range on Puttenham Common, to which we were taken by bus. It was a pretty boring occupation, bound up with the O.T.C., which meant that for competitions with other schools, and for the famous Ashburton Shield at Bisley, we had to wear our O.T.C. uniforms. This I hated, particularly the puttees on one's legs, and the awful round cap.

One of my companions in the VIII was John Derry, who became a close friend. Obviously, I had no idea then, nor had he, that he would become the famous test pilot for de Havillands and die at the Farnborough Air Show, when his plane broke up at speed, and crashed into the crowd.

When I visit Charterhouse now, I like to see his photograph at the workshops, dedicated to his memory.

Several of the masters, who taught us, had been in the Army in the 1914/18 war, and told us terrible stories about trench warfare

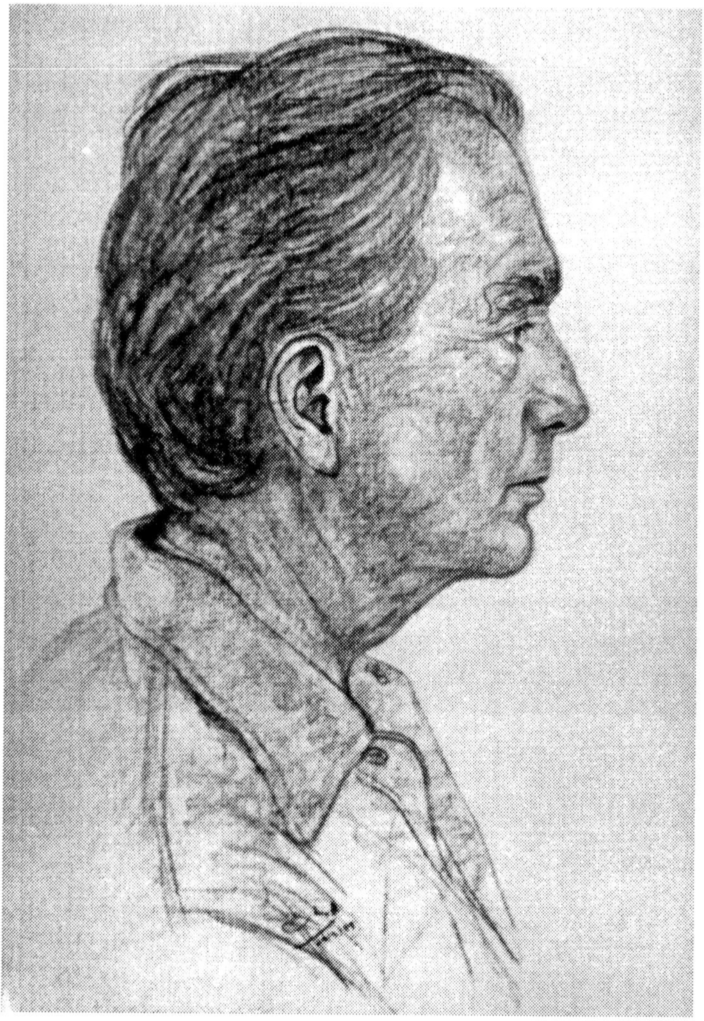

Lieutenant Michael Bray, DSC RNVR

in France. For this reason, I vowed that if war came (and in 1938, after digging trenches near the Chapel, war seemed a distinct possibility) I would try and avoid joining the Army at all costs, and when an "R.A.F. Section" of the O.T.C. was formed, I eagerly joined that. "Field Days" were then much more fun, as we were taken to R.A.F. Odiham, and flew in Ansons and Lysanders.

I also had a short spell in the "Corps Band", as a drummer – anything to avoid the "P.B.I."!

When the war did come in September 1939, I didn't go to Cambridge, but joined the Navy as an Ordinary Seaman – at least there were no muddy trenches or barbed wire, but I found that, instead, there was seasickness, crowded mess decks, and sleeping in a hammock (it was at these times that I wished that I was at Cambridge). However, I survived, and spent nearly seven very formative years in the Navy, which I now regard as having been my university.

A Motor Gunboat

Whilst my memory was reasonably fresh, I wrote a small book about my Naval Service, called "One Young Man's War (1939–1946), and I quote from it, so that modern Carthusians can understand what it was like to be pitched out of the secure life in Gownboys, to the precarious life of a seaman, later an officer, in the wartime Navy.

At the age of eighteen, I didn't have to join any of the Services, as conscription only came in at the age of twenty, several years later, but I felt disorientated by what was happening around me, and going up to Cambridge seemed pointless. I also felt slightly ashamed, I think, that some members of older generations than mine had, through a much publicised Oxford Union vote, declared by a majority that "they would not fight for King and Country". I suppose that I was more idealistic and aware that, as I had had a more privileged upbringing than the majority of my age in England, I should try and set an example. Priggish perhaps, but that was sixty years ago, and attitudes were different then.

After a short spell at sea in a destroyer, I was sent to Portland for a three months course to train me to become an anti-submarine detection operator, which then became my job in a destroyer on Atlantic Convoy work. We made at least one "kill".

In April 1940, we, with several other destroyers, were sent to Dover to form the Dover Patrol (the name of the game that we played before the days of "Monopoly"). We were then in the period of the "phoney war" when nothing much was happening between the Allies and the Germans.

Suddenly, on May 10th 1940, everything changed overnight, when the Germans invaded the Low Countries, and we found ourselves with troops and a demolition party on board, proceeding at full speed to the Hook of Holland, and up the River Maas, to where the German parachute troops were dropping into the bulb fields around us, and we were being attacked by German planes. Having landed our troops, we spent several dangerous days there, and were then recalled to Chatham. There, I received the welcome news that I was being sent to a Naval Shore Base at Hove, in Sussex, to be trained for a commission, and three months later, I emerged as a Midshipman.

My first appointment was to an "Armed Merchant Cruiser" doing convoy protection work, between Glasgow and Gibraltar.

She was a beautiful passenger liner called "*Cilicia*", and had been fitted with eight old six inch guns, and whilst practising celestial navigation on these voyages, we hoped that we would not be victims of attack by German U-boats or surface vessels, because we were almost a sitting duck.

But it was nice to reach Gibraltar, with all its lights (after the British blackout) and better weather than Glasgow.

At this time the Admiralty had organised a programme to build many wooden fast patrol boats, for inshore convoy work, and every yacht yard around the U.K. was engaged in building these M.L.s. I was appointed as the second officer to one of these boats, building in Cornwall. From there I was eventually appointed to Motor Gunboats (very fast, offensive vessels, equipped with guns rather than torpedoes, to fight marauding German E-boats, who were attacking our coastal convoys with torpedoes), and with my commanding officer, a young Canadian from Vancouver, we collected our first boat from Liverpool, to which it had been shipped, on lend-lease from the American Navy, and thus commenced a very exciting period of some two years, based at Dover and Ramsgate, in which, whilst still only twenty, I eventually had command of a Motor Gun Boat, in a flotilla of eight boats.

I quote from my book, an account of a night action on April 4th, 1943 (my 22nd birthday, and the day that Bill Moss, my old school friend, was landing in Crete, to capture his General).

> "We set out at dusk for the Belgian coast, Dick Richards[1] in the lead, and supported by ourselves and MGB 117 making

[1] Lieut. G.D.K. Richards, D.S.O., D.S.C., R.N.

up the three boat unit. Once we were across on the other side, we reduced speed on to silent engines, and crept up the swept channel with our rather primitive radar searching the sea ahead.

It must have been around midnight when we detected something near us. We would have communicated with each other by shouting from boat to boat, and Dick would have said "We'll investigate this contact, stand by to attack", and on board, we would tell the gun crews where to expect to see their targets, and we would scan the horizon with our night glasses.

When we eventually made out their dark shapes in the blackness (I can't remember whether there were two or three) we realised they were probably flak trawlers on patrol, and we had surprised them.

As soon as we had got close to them, Dick's boat opened fire on the nearest ship and increased speed, and we all followed suit. The enemy ship took a terrible pounding from our three boats, but the other vessels were now firing accurately at us, but they then turned away and increased speed, leaving our target stopped and burning.

We made another run on our target, and now her guns were no longer firing, and we could hear cries in the water alongside her. Her crew were abandoning her. Dick's voice came across the water, "pick up the survivors, and we will board her, and try and get a tow rope on her".

It is difficult to remember what happened next, but we picked up one survivor from the water, and then went alongside the ship, and Bill[2] and some of our crew jumped on board, and after what seemed ages to me wondering whether we would be attacked in this very vulnerable position, Bill came back with the trawler's signal and

[2] Lieut. W.L. Fesq, D.S.C., R.A.N.V.R.

code books, and various other trophies.

In the meantime, Dick had decided that the fires on board were so serious that it was unlikely that we could tow the vessel back to Dover, we had our own damage and casualties, and it was best to sink her and return home.

First of all we took stock of our own position. We had sustained many hits, our front gunner, A/B Jane, was dead, shot through the head, and several others were slightly wounded. There was a large shell hole in the side of the boat, where our petrol tanks were, and a smell of burning, in addition to other damage to the hull and superstructure.

This was when Bill performed a very brave action – he volunteered to hang head down over the side where the shell hole was, and, with an extinguisher, put out any fire there. So we held him by his legs, until he reported that the tanks did not appear to be holed, and that the hole was well above the water-line.

Dick's voice came across the water, "our motor mechanic has been aboard the trawler and opened the sea cocks, but she doesn't seem to be filling very fast. We can't leave her in case the enemy comes back, so we must try and sink her with depth charges".

Then 110 dropped a charge as she steamed past the stricken vessel, but it was too far away to do much damage. "113 it's your turn next and you must try and get it underneath her hull."

I knew that the only effective way to do this was literally to go alongside her and drop our charge from a stopped position, and risk being blown up as well, if we didn't get away quickly enough.

We normally envisaged dropping our charges in front of a moving ship, so that the explosion would be underneath, and in order to delay the depth charge pistol (which is operated by water pressure) we had an empty oil barrel on a

50ft line attached to the charge, to prevent the charge sinking too fast.

This was fine in more normal circumstances, but dropped from a standstill, the wire could get hooked up on a deck fitting or round one of the propellers, when we would be "hoist by our own petard". I therefore cautioned Bill to double check that the line was clear of everything, and then we slowly proceeded alongside the ship's side, bumped it a number of times, and when we were amidships, I shouted "O.K. Bill", and then, a few seconds later, slammed the throttles open. Bill had done a thorough job – the depth charge didn't follow us, and 113 leapt away like a scalded cat. As we sped away we looked aft, there was an explosion which seemed to lift the trawler slowly up in the air, and then she dropped back, her keel broken, and began to settle quickly.

After a while we started back on the long haul to Ramsgate, exhilarated by our successful action, but suddenly very tired and anxious that it could all have gone wrong, and that we might have been like the wet shivering prisoner on our foredeck, whom we had forgotten in the general excitement.

It was on another patrol one night, off Cap Gris Nez, looking for enemy shipping, that we had a very narrow escape. We were with Dick Richards leading, and Ronnie Barge[3] in line astern and at half speed, when we felt a terrible bump on our bow which made the whole boat shudder. I throttled down and immediately thought of mines (we had recently lost a boat, blown in half by a mine) but it must have been a large piece of wreckage.

When the boat had stopped, Bill went forward and reported that we were badly holed in the forepeak, and making water.

[3] Lieut. R.M. Barge, D.S.C., R.N.V.R.

The other two boats had by then disappeared into the darkness, unaware of what had happened to us until we were able to radio them, and then they couldn't find us.

It was only slowly that we realised the full horror of our plight. We were on our own, only miles from the French coast. We were so far down by the bow that our stern was partly out of the water, which meant that the cooling water inlets for the engines were also out of the water, and that we couldn't run the engines, so we couldn't get under way and head for home, and with the main engines out of action, we had no hydraulic power for the gun turrets, so we couldn't defend ourselves, other than with the bridge machine guns. We managed to get a wireless signal through to Dover, and then all we could do was to wait and see what would happen – perhaps the Germans would send a patrol boat out to get us. It began to get light, and soon we could see the headland of Cap Gris Nez quite clearly. Some of the crew said – looking at the coast – "at least we aren't too far from home". Bill and I decided not to tell them it wasn't home!

The sea was calm, and we lay quietly in a slight swell. Suddenly there was a "whooshing" noise, an explosion, and a great spout of water.

We all knew what that was, and there was nothing we could do about it either. Shelling from the shore batteries continued for some time, I don't remember for how long, but whilst some shells landed quite close, we were not hit or damaged.

And then we were suddenly cheered up, as two fighters appeared overhead and circled us, their pilots waving. They were RAF Typhoons and we were no longer alone, our morale went up. They would report our position and protect us. But the interlude was all too short. The shelling had stopped, and then out of the blue came the Messerschmitts. We had hardly realised what was happening when we suddenly saw both our Typhoon escorts dive into the sea, as they were jumped by the Germans, out of the sun.

Both pilots must have been killed instantly, and we felt awful that they had died violent deaths for us. And then it was our turn – flying low over the sea, their eight guns firing, the sea around us erupted into spray, and there was nothing we could do other than fire off our inadequate machine guns.

After several runs at us, they disappeared and it was eerily quiet again.

Bill, as one would expect, was cool and collected. We surveyed the boat for damage, which was only slight, and luckily we were all uninjured, but shaken. What was going to happen next?

I don't remember how long afterwards it was, but we gradually became aware of more planes above us, and then we realised that they were ours. The RAF, angered by the loss of its Typhoons, was putting an "umbrella" above us, and then it was that we spotted on the horizon, coming towards us from England, two of our boats at speed.

It was Dick Richards and Ronnie Barge coming back to find us, and what a welcome sight they were.

They soon closed us, a tow rope was secured, and we began the long slow haul back to home and safety, while the RAF seemed to fill the sky above us.

Once through the gap in the minefield, a tug was waiting to take over the tow, and we made faster progress back to Dover, and as we came through the harbour entrance, a message from the Admiral was flashed to us – "Welcome home"."

In the autumn of 1943, I was appointed to a Fleet Destroyer, still building at Birkenhead – the First Lieutenant was to be Lt Norman Macpherson D.S.C., R.N., who had been my MGB Flotilla Senior Officer at Lowestoft. HMS *Undaunted* was a fine ship, and I was with her for over two years – for the Normandy Landings at the Second Front, in the Mediterranean, the Indian Ocean, and finally with the British Pacific Fleet, part of U.S. Task Force 57, winning the Sea War against the Japanese.

Of the Normandy landings in 1944, I wrote the following in my book:

> "That spring the Flotilla was ordered down to the south coast of England where the invasion fleet was being assembled in all the various harbours along the south coast and primarily in the Solent. Our Flotilla was to anchor off Yarmouth in the Isle of Wight, an area which I knew well from my sailing days as a boy. It was an amazing sight, ships everywhere, and a sense of excitement and foreboding as we realised that this was the invasion fleet to take the Allied armies back into France.
>
> The scale of the operation and the organisation behind it was quite incredible and a few days before D-day we were given our confidential briefing of our role.
>
> We were to cross over before the landing craft and arrive at our station off the coast at dawn, where we were to anchor, just off the shore, and to engage with our guns specified targets such as gun emplacements on the beach, which would have hindered our troops landing. We were given very detailed photographs of our stretch of shoreline taken at wave top height by Spitfires with cameras in their wings and each of our targets was numbered and clearly identified. To seaward of us would be the cruisers and bigger ships which would engage the German shore batteries with their bigger guns. Once the naval force had accomplished their job, the landing craft would come through and land their troops. It sounded very hazardous for us.
>
> There were several days to go before D-day, and I remember going ashore at Yarmouth and walking up the

little lanes behind the town, which were fresh and green with spring flowers and foliage, the English countryside at its best. I remember wondering whether I would see it again.

The day before we were due to leave, the weather suddenly went bad, it blew a gale, and everybody became very worried. Then a patrol vessel with a loud hailer ran through the lines of ships broadcasting the message that Operation Overlord was postponed for 24 hours. It was a considerable anticlimax.

However, the next day the weather had improved and that evening we hauled up our anchor and slipped out through the Needles channel and set course for France at slow speed.

I remember that it was a quiet night, and rather than try and catch a few hours' sleep in my cabin aft, I stayed on deck and sat with my back to the superstructure, just above the fo'c'sle break, watching the sea go by, and wondering what was awaiting us.

In the early hours we closed up at action stations, and noticed a lot of air activity over the Cherbourg peninsula, which was drawing anti-aircraft fire from the Germans. This was the initial parachute force going in to drop behind the lines, together with the troop-filled gliders towed by their aircraft tugs. Ahead of us was the French coast but it was all quiet.

As the sky began to lighten in the east, we slipped into our position off our beach in the Bay of the Seine, and I was sent forward to anchor the ship with my Fo'c'sle party. We must have been spotted by the Germans at this time, because there were gun flashes behind the coast and then shells began to drop around us. I felt very naked up on the fo'c'sle.

It was getting light by now and we could see our targets just as they were shown in the photographs that we had been given, and immediately we started firing our main armament at our targets on the beach and cliffs. Luckily the cruisers to seaward of us had also started to fire at the shore batteries which were shelling us, and in a short while they had been silenced and were no longer worrying us.

It was then that hundreds of landing craft appeared from seaward, and passing us, their troops waving, they beached themselves on the sand, and the troops were able to get ashore without too many casualties and establish themselves.

Initially there were some air attacks on the fleet and the beaches, but after a bit our own aircraft seemed to get control of the air and we were not unduly molested.

"Footprints in Time", by Sir John Colville, gives a vivid account of how he saw the invasion fleet from his fighter plane.

> "At 3.00 a.m. I was awoken for briefing. The skies had cleared and in the early light I set off with one accompanying aircraft to perform a tactical reconnaissance of an area in Normandy near Falaise. As we set course for Selsey Bill, flying over the somnolent Hampshire villages and fields flecked by the rising sun, it was impossible not to feel exultantly melodramatic and I doubt if I was the only pilot that morning who told himself with commonplace self-satisfaction that 'Gentlemen in England, now a-bed, shall think themselves accursed they were not here, and hold their manhood cheap . . .' I even wished it were St Crispin's Day.
>
> "The Channel was teeming with ships: convoys of landing craft, large and small; big troop-ships; destroyers and cruisers: thousands of ships with their white bow-waves and thousands of barrage balloons. In the sky we mingled with an equally vast array of Spitfires and Typhoons of the RAF and Lightnings and Thunderbolts of the US Army Air Force. We were in the van of the greatest Crusade of all times, elated to the extent of spiritual intoxication, and so instilled with a sense of unity with those thousands of others who

> were setting forth on the same venture that the hazards ahead were of no consequence, and fear was a forgotten emotion. War in these conditions is, for a short span, magnificent.
>
> "A long line of men-of-war lay off the Normandy coast, their big naval guns blazing and the burst of their shells inland distinctly visible. The trajectory of their missiles was high and that very morning one of my brother officers in 168 Squadron was struck by a 15" shell from the Warspite, he and his plane entirely disintegrating. The chances of being hit by a 15" shell when flying at 5000 feet must be small indeed."

All through that amazing day waves of landing craft continued to arrive, our Gunnery Liaison Officer, Captain Remington Hobbs, went ashore and we were able to support the advancing troops with our gunfire directed by him, by radio. There were also some amazing sights as the concrete sections of the Mulberry harbours began to arrive, towed by tugs and put into position, and later on extraordinary contraptions called PLUTO (Pipe Line under the Ocean) which were huge floating drums of hosepipe, towed by tugs, which were unrolling miles of petrol hose across the Channel and were the means of supply of petrol to the army when they got ashore.

By the evening things were comparatively quiet in our sector as the batteries and coastal defences had been silenced and the troops had been able to advance several miles inland, and there wasn't much enemy air activity. Luckily we were all on a considerable "high", so that exhaustion hadn't caught up with us and we were able to go back to a two watch system and get some food and rest.

The next day (D+1), we proceeded westward parallel to the beach, to see what was going on, when we were suddenly hailed by one of the Navy's fast minelayers, HMS *Apollo*. She called us up on her lamp to say that unfortunately she had run aground, and she had on board some VIPs, who had to be taken back to

Portsmouth, and we were to take them on board.

We were surprised and delighted to find that the VIPs were General Eisenhower, the Commander in Chief of the whole operation and Admiral Ramsay who was the Commander in Chief of All Naval Forces, together with their staffs. They had been reconnoitring the beachhead on board *Apollo* when unfortunately she hit a sandbank and lost a propeller.

They came on board and had a quick glass of sherry in the wardroom and then went up to the bridge when we set course for Portsmouth at high speed.

As soon as we discovered who we had on board, we had to make a Five Star General's flag and hoist it to the masthead as we steamed through the fleet, which was very satisfactory as every ship that we passed and which we would normally have had to salute as they were senior to us, now had to salute us. General Eisenhower was very nice and friendly and spoke to everyone, and was able to tell us that the landing was going well, and we duly put them all ashore in Portsmouth Harbour.

By chance last year I read an obituary in the Daily Telegraph of a Captain J. Grindle, who had been the Captain of the *Apollo* at the time, and must have had a most ghastly experience when he ran his ship aground. The obituary contained a reference to this incident and the relevant portion is as follows:

> "Captain John Grindle, who has died aged 90, successfully overcame one of the most unfortunate mishaps ever to befall a naval officer.
>
> "In 1944 he took command of *Apollo*, a brand new 40-knot minelayer, and was mentioned in despatches for the ship's part in laying defensive minefields in the English Channel in April and May 1944 to guard the Normandy assault area against U-boats.
>
> "But on D-Day plus-one, June 7, the ship left Portsmouth for a tour of inspection of the Normandy beaches, having

embarked a party that included the Supreme Allied Commander, Gen Eisenhower, and the Allied Naval Commander, Adml Sir Bertram Ramsay, together with members of their staffs.

"Off Normandy, Rear Adml Sir Philip Vian, commanding the Eastern Task Force, and Cdre Douglas-Pennant, commanding the assault force for Gold Beach, also came on board, making *Apollo*'s bridge so crowded that Grindle sent his navigating officer to the wheelhouse below. This may have had some bearing on what was to follow.

"*Apollo* was steaming close inshore when she went the wrong side of a buoy and ran aground on a sand bar. Capt Grindle boldly chose not to stop but to force the ship over. "With much shuddering of the hull and whipping of the mast, he succeeded in this intention, at the cost of one propeller torn off and another shaft bent. *Apollo* disembarked her VIPs into another ship and went home at six knots.

"By an extraordinary coincidence the destroyer taking Gen Montgomery on a similar tour of the beaches, also ran aground the next day, but Grindle was too generous a spirit to take any comfort from that.

"Gen. Eisenhower felt that he had in some way been responsible for what happened, and wrote a letter of mitigation to the First Sea Lord on Grindle's behalf. Grindle was none the less reprimanded by a court martial – after which one flag officer said to him, 'Join the club: we've all been reprimanded.' "

After the landings in Normandy were more established, our Destroyer Flotilla was sent down to the Mediterranean, and to the Adriatic, to give bombardment support to the Allied Armies, making their slow way up the coasts of Italy.

From there we went through the Suez Canal into the Indian Ocean, to the big Naval Base of Trincomalee, in Ceylon, where the British Pacific Fleet was assembling. This consisted of four big Fleet Aircraft Carriers, four Battleships, eight Cruisers and sixteen Destroyers – a formidable force,but small compared to the U.S. Pacific Fleet, which we were to join.

From there the Fleet sailed to Australia, bombarding and bombing oil installations in Sumatra, on the way, despite attacks by Japanese torpedo bombers, a foretaste of things to come from our new enemies.

The Fleet was based at Sydney, and we went to sea for long periods, up to three months in the vast area of the Pacific, and this was made possible by the "Fleet Train", a fleet of merchant ships carrying provisions and supplies, oil tankers from which we refuelled, and small aircraft carriers, carrying replacement aircraft and pilots, for the big carriers. The Americans had a similar but much bigger "Armada". The "Fleet Trains" stayed in convoy, about 500 miles to seaward of the Operational Fleet.

The Combined Fleet could fly off hundreds of attack aircraft against the Japanese, and the big guns of the battleships were used to bombard the mainland, but our worst enemy was the Kamikaze Japanese suicide bomber, who went for the carriers, and did a lot of damage. Eventually the Japanese capitulated in August 1945.

After a short spell in hospital in Sydney, en route to Hong Kong from Auckland, New Zealand, where we had had a refit, I was sent home in a Frigate to Portsmouth, for demobilisation in May 1946.

I was offered a job with a firm of Insurance Brokers at Lloyd's of London, at an annual salary of £200. I didn't think much of this salary, but as I could live at home, I took it, and I found, to my surprise, that it was very interesting, and when I worked as a Broker in the Underwriting Room, which was like a large market place, full of people making bargains with each other, I found lots of young men of my own age, who had been in the Services, and so we had much in common. Lloyd's has many Clubs and associations for the people working there, and I was soon a member of Lloyd's Yacht Club, and got many opportunities to crew in Ocean Racers owned by people in the market. When Lloyd's decided to build a Class I Ocean Racer, and enter her in the prestigious Newport, U.S.A., to Bermuda Race, I was offered a place in the crew of all Lloyd's men. It was a wonderful opportunity. We were given three months paid leave, "*Lutine*" was shipped to Long Island, and we followed in the "*Queen Mary*".

There were ten of us, plus a hand on board, and we took part in many regattas, showing the Lloyd's flag, and eventually the Bermuda race. Unfortunately, partly due to being a new boat and having teething troubles, we didn't do very well, and after a spell on that lovely island, we took part in one of the first transatlantic races, back to Plymouth. It took 23 days, and was a great experience.

As I became more senior, I was sent abroad on business to service clients and get new business, and these visits took me, not only to Europe, but to the Middle East, East and South Africa, and to Australia. I loved it. In due course, I did my stint as the Deputy Chairman, and Chairman of the Lloyd's Insurance Brokers Association, and, in the 1970's, I instigated and helped carry through, a merger with another Lloyd's Broking Company, and we obtained a quotation on the London Stock Exchange.

The Firm grew, there were other mergers and takeovers, and now, in 1999, the Firm that I started with is part of a huge world wide organisation called Willis Corroon, and things are very different in the Lloyd's Market.

Our retirement age was 60 in those days, and when I was 58, and saw which way things were going, I volunteered to go to Bermuda, for two years, to start up and run a Financial Management Company for our Group.

Bermuda, at that time, was becoming a centre for Reinsurance Companies, owned by big U.S. Industrial and other International Companies, as there were certain taxation and accounting benefits to be had, and as insurance expertise was needed, the big Lloyd's and U.S. Brokers were getting in on the act by forming Bermuda Companies, and staffing them from London and New York. My colleagues were a bit surprised by my idea, but agreed, and Paula and I duly moved to Bermuda in 1978. We didn't know it at the time, but it was a watershed in our lives, because we never returned to live in England!

After my two year contract expired, I and my company were happy to carry on, and so we did, for several more years, before we retired, to live mainly in France in 1986. The reinsurance market in Bermuda is now huge.

We both loved the sun and the sea, which led us to make two unfortunate but enjoyable investments.

The first was a small beach house on a tiny island in the British Virgin Islands. The island had no water, electricity, roads, shops, or public communications with the outside world, but it had beautiful sandy beaches, a small mountain and about 100 inhabitants. It was romantic and idyllic for us, and we bought a motor boat, to get us there from the U.S. island of St. Thomas. We had it for holidays for three wonderful years, until it got burnt down by persons unknown, when we were back in Bermuda. We were so unhappy, but the wreck was eventually bought by an American couple, who wanted somewhere safe against nuclear fall out, and, with the insurance money, we came out all square – we were lucky.

Then we fell for the island of Montserrat in the Caribbean, after visiting friends there, and bought a small house on a cliff above the sea. After I retired, we used to go there from January to April each year, and it was a lovely "other life" to France.

We were able to fly from France to Guadaloupe and then hop across to Montserrat.

Unfortunately, in 1996, and without any warning, a small extinct volcano on the island became active again, after some 400 years, destroying about two-thirds of the island, but not our house, and we haven't been able to go back since. We have allowed a homeless local family to live in our house and look after it.

Maybe one day, we shall be able to go back.

CHAPTER III

"Sic Transit Gloria . . ."

Ralph has often said to me, "I have been very lucky", but he was also very capable. Bill was also lucky to survive some of his adventures, but unlucky to die young. I consider myself to have been lucky too, especially as I am now living in retirement in S.W. France, in an old stone farmhouse, with a view of the Pyrenees in the distance, and lovely rolling farmlands and wooded hills in between. We came here, partly by chance, and partly because Paula is a francophile and has had a house in France before. I have some french genes from my mother's Huguenot family, who came from France to England, in 1699.

I would like to know what happened to Sophie Moss and her two children, and maybe this book will reach someone who does know, and can tell me.

That Bill and his family went to live in Jamaica may be more than a coincidence, as Ian Fleming, the creator of James Bond, also lived there, and worked in Intelligence in the war. Bill would have made a good Bond – he even had the looks.

Ralph and Ann live in their large apartment, a stone's throw from the steps of Westminster Cathedral, surrounded by books and pictures, and they spend some time also at their cottage on the shores of Chichester Harbour.

Ralph and I see each other occasionally in London.

I have three children and nine grandchildren. I am now 78, and hope that I will see more years, because my father died in his 94th year, and I still have lots of things to do.

Speaking for all three of us, I think that Charterhouse did us well, and that we, in our turn, have done well, for the reputation of Charterhouse.

Two Charterhouse Families

Francis Evelyn Bray	1880–1973	Girdlestoneites
Lt.Col. Frederick Richard Chancourt Bray	1913–1991	Gownboys
The Rev. Anthony Markham Bray	1916–1999	Gownboys
Francis Arthur Michael Bray	1921–	Gownboys
Francis Ian Richard Bray	1942–1998	Gownboys
Elspeth Bray (née Moncrieff)	1959–	Gownboys
Neville Charles Chancourt Girardot	1925	Weekites
Edward Paul Chancourt Girardot	1954–	Weekites

The Brays and Girardots are first cousins.

The Houses at Charterhouse in 1939

Saunderites
Verites
Gownboys
Girdlestoneites (also known as Duckites)
Lockites
Weekites
Hodgsonites
Daviesites
Bodeites
Pageites
Robinites

Bibliography

"Ill met by Moonlight" by W. Stanley MOSS
"A War of Shadows" by W. Stanley MOSS
"One Young Man's War (1939–1946)" by Michael BRAY

(All the above books are in the Charterhouse Library)